BY

Elizabeth Baird

AND

The Food Writers of Canadian Living Magazine
and The Canadian Living Test Kitchen

A MADISON PRESS BOOK

PRODUCED FOR

BALLANTINE BOOKS AND CANADIAN LIVING™

Ballantine Books
A Division of
Random House of
Canada Limited
1265 Aerowood Drive
Mississauga, Ontario
Canada
L4W 1B9

Canadian Living
Telemedia
Communications Inc.
25 Sheppard Avenue West
Suite 100
North York, Ontario
Canada
M2N 6S7

Canadian Cataloguing in Publication Data

Muffins & more

(Canadian Living's best)
ISBN 0-345-39800-9

1. Muffins. 2. Baking.
I. Baird, Elizabeth. II. Series.

TX770.M84 1994 641.815 C94-930272-4

EDITORIAL DIRECTOR: Hugh Brewster
PROJECT EDITOR: Wanda Nowakowska
EDITORIAL ASSISTANCE: Beverley Renahan
PRODUCTION DIRECTOR: Susan Barrable
PRODUCTION COORDINATOR: Donna Chong
BOOK DESIGN AND LAYOUT: Gordon Sibley Design Inc.
COLOR SEPARATION: Colour Technologies
PRINTING AND BINDING: Friesen Printers

CANADIAN LIVING ADVISORY BOARD: Elizabeth Baird, Bonnie Baker Cowan, Anna Hobbs, Caren King, Greg MacNeil, Kirk Shearer

CANADIAN LIVING'S™ BEST MUFFINS & MORE
was produced by Madison Press Books
under the direction of Albert E. Cummings

Madison Press Books
40 Madison Avenue
Toronto, Ontario, Canada
M5R 2S1

Printed in Canada

Contents

Introduction

When we surveyed Canadians to find out whether they bake at home, and why, we kept hearing the same answers over and over again.

While saving money might be the obvious reason for making your own easy baking, it isn't the most important reason why more and more Canadians are baking their own muffins, cookies, biscuits and no-fuss cakes.

For starters, you told us home baking simply tastes better. You get to choose your own ingredients — the finest, freshest available that will deliver maximum flavor — and you can tailor your baking to suit your household. You can substitute fruits and nuts according to taste and the stock in your cupboard, and opt for healthier recipes with bran, whole wheat flour and yogurt. Home baking gives you control.

Most importantly, and in overwhelming numbers, we discovered Canadians also bake simply for the pleasure it gives them. It may be corny to equate home baking with love, but most of us associate sweet food with the most heart-felt occasions. What would Christmas be without cookies, or Jewish New Year bereft of honey cake, birthdays without a candle-lit cake or cupcake, fund-raising for a favored project deprived of at least one bake sale?

This is baking at its most uncomplicated, with readily available ingredients and minimal equipment — baking that fits into a Saturday morning or a weeknight, with members of the household lending a hand. And that's exactly what you'll find in *Canadian Living's Best Muffins & More.*

Baking just the way you want it, with delicious results!

Elizabeth Baird

Hot Cross Muffins
(recipe, p. 8)

Muffin Magic

The secret of a good muffin is fresh-from-the-oven flavor — a freshness that's easy to get because muffins take so little time to mix together. Here's our pick of the very best sweet and savory muffins.

Sticky Almond Muffins ▸

These rich muffins are perfect for brunch parties or come-over-for-coffee affairs.

3/4 cup	sliced almonds	175 mL
1/2 cup	packed brown sugar	125 mL
1/2 cup	butter, melted	125 mL
2 cups	all-purpose flour	500 mL
2 tsp	baking powder	10 mL
1/2 tsp	baking soda	2 mL
1/2 tsp	salt	2 mL
2	eggs	2
1 cup	sour cream	250 mL
1/2 tsp	vanilla	2 mL
1/2 tsp	almond extract	2 mL

● Toast almonds on baking sheet in 350°F (180°C) oven for about 10 minutes or until golden brown. Divide 2 tsp (10 mL) among 12 well-greased or nonstick muffin cups; sprinkle each with 1 tsp (5 mL) of the sugar. Drizzle each with 2 tsp (10 mL) of the butter. Set aside.

● In large bowl, combine flour, remaining sugar, remaining almonds, baking powder, baking soda and salt. Whisk together eggs, remaining butter, sour cream, vanilla and almond extract; pour over dry ingredients. Stir together just until moistened.

● Spoon into prepared muffin cups. Bake in 375°F (190°C) oven for 20 to 25 minutes or until golden brown and tops are firm to the touch. Let stand in pan on rack for 5 minutes. Remove from pan, scraping any glazed almonds in pan onto bottoms of muffins. Let cool, upside down, on rack for 3 minutes. Serve warm. Makes 12 muffins.

Fresh Ginger Muffins

Muffins are served up for weekend brunch in many restaurants across Canada, including the Backstreet Café in Meaford, Ontario, where these lemon-ginger ones are always a hit.

1/4 cup	minced gingerroot	50 mL
1 cup	granulated sugar	250 mL
2 tbsp	grated lemon rind	25 mL
1/2 cup	butter	125 mL
2	eggs	2
2 cups	all-purpose flour	500 mL
3/4 tsp	baking soda	4 mL
1/2 tsp	salt	2 mL
1 cup	buttermilk	250 mL

● In skillet, cook ginger and 1/4 cup (50 mL) of the sugar over low heat, stirring, for about 3 minutes or until melted. Let cool. Stir in lemon rind and 1/4 cup (50 mL) more sugar.

● In large bowl, beat butter with remaining sugar; beat in eggs, one at a time. Stir in ginger mixture. Combine flour, baking soda and salt; stir into butter mixture alternately with buttermilk, making three additions of dry and two of buttermilk.

● Spoon into greased or paper-lined muffin cups. Bake in 375°F (190°C) oven for 20 to 25 minutes or until tops are firm to the touch. Makes 8 muffins.

Hot Cross Muffins

With the delicious look and spicy taste of yeast-raised hot cross buns — but muffin-quick and muffin-easy — these little gems are a treat any time of the year. *(photo, p. 4)*

2 cups	all-purpose flour	500 mL
1 cup	currants	250 mL
1/2 cup	granulated sugar	125 mL
2 tsp	baking powder	10 mL
1 tsp	cinnamon	5 mL
1/2 tsp	nutmeg	2 mL
1/2 tsp	ground cloves	2 mL
1/2 tsp	baking soda	2 mL
1/2 tsp	salt	2 mL
2	eggs	2
1 cup	milk	250 mL
1/4 cup	vegetable oil	50 mL
2 tbsp	grated orange rind	25 mL
1 cup	sifted icing sugar	250 mL
4 tsp	(approx) water	20 mL

● In large bowl, combine flour, currants, granulated sugar, baking powder, cinnamon, nutmeg, cloves, baking soda and salt. Whisk together eggs, milk, oil and orange rind; pour over dry ingredients. Stir together just until moistened.

● Spoon into greased or paper-lined muffin cups. Bake in 400°F (200°C) oven for about 20 minutes or until tops are firm to the touch. Let cool.

● Whisk together icing sugar and water, adding up to 1 tsp (5 mL) more water if necessary to make creamy consistency. Pipe or drizzle to form X over top of each muffin. Makes 12 muffins.

Eggnog Muffins

Let the vibrant flavor of nutmeg sing out in a party muffin.

1/2 cup	golden raisins	125 mL
1/2 cup	dark rum	125 mL
2 cups	all-purpose flour	500 mL
3/4 cup	granulated sugar	175 mL
2 tsp	baking powder	10 mL
1-1/4 tsp	nutmeg	6 mL
1/2 tsp	baking soda	2 mL
1/2 tsp	salt	2 mL
1 cup	sour cream	250 mL
2	eggs	2
1/4 cup	butter, melted	50 mL
1 tsp	vanilla	5 mL

● In small bowl, combine raisins and rum; set aside.

● In large bowl, combine flour, sugar, baking powder, 1 tsp (5 mL) of the nutmeg, baking soda and salt. Whisk together sour cream, eggs, butter and vanilla; pour over dry ingredients. Pour raisin mixture over top; stir just until dry ingredients are moistened.

● Spoon into greased or paper-lined muffin cups. Sprinkle with remaining nutmeg. Bake in 400°F (200°C) oven for about 20 minutes or until golden brown and tops are firm to the touch. Makes 12 muffins.

TIP: Nutmeg adds a distinctive flavor to eggnog, and freshly grated nutmeg gives the optimum zing. Buy whole nutmeg and grate the spice as needed — on a curved nutmeg grater or on the fine grate of a regular square grater.

DRIED FRUIT AND NUT SUBSTITUTIONS

● One of the best things about muffin recipes is their versatility. Most dried fruit — raisins, currants, dried apricots, prunes, pears, peaches, dates and figs (snip off the hard tip first) — can be used interchangeably. The new dried fruits such as dried cherries, blueberries and cranberries are also excellent muffin ingredients.

● Most unsalted nuts — pecans, walnuts, hazelnuts, almonds and Brazil nuts — are also interchangeable. When buying walnuts, choose plump, golden, fresh-tasting ones from bulk food outlets, or pick up California walnuts in bags and vacuum containers.

Blueberry Orange Muffins

1-3/4 cups	all-purpose flour	425 mL
2/3 cup	packed brown sugar	150 mL
1 tbsp	baking powder	15 mL
1 tbsp	grated orange rind	15 mL
1 cup	milk	250 mL
2	eggs	2
3 tbsp	butter, melted	50 mL
1 tsp	vanilla	5 mL
1 cup	blueberries	250 mL

● In large bowl, combine flour, sugar, baking powder and orange rind. Whisk together milk, eggs, butter and vanilla; pour over dry ingredients. Sprinkle with blueberries; stir just until dry ingredients are moistened.

● Spoon into greased or paper-lined muffin cups. Bake in 400°F (200°C) oven for 20 to 25 minutes or until golden and tops are firm to the touch. Makes 10 large muffins.

VARIATION

● RASPBERRY STREUSEL MUFFINS: ▲ Replace blueberries with raspberries; increase butter to 1/4 cup (50 mL). For topping, stir together 1/4 cup (50 mL) packed brown sugar, 2 tbsp (25 mL) all-purpose flour and 1/4 tsp (1 mL) cinnamon. Drizzle with 1 tbsp (15 mL) melted butter and toss with fork to combine. Sprinkle over batter before baking muffins.

Blueberry muffins are a Canadian classic, worth serving often, especially in blueberry season and when company comes from afar. For a change of taste, substitute raspberries for the blueberries and add a satisfying streusel topping — as we did for the photo above.

TIP: For superior flavor, always choose the smaller low-bush blueberries, often called wild blueberries. Fresh, they add a punch of color and taste to a muffin. Frozen, blueberries will turn muffin batter green if allowed to thaw or if stirred too much.

MUFFIN BAKING EQUIPMENT

You don't need much in the way of equipment to get muffins underway. The following items are helpful.

- Two mixing bowls — one larger for dry ingredients, one smaller for liquids and eggs.
- Measuring cups — nesting measures for dry ingredients and spouted glass cups for liquids.
- Measuring spoons.
- Chopping board and knife for cutting nuts and fruit.
- Large wooden spoon for stirring batter.
- Rubber spatula for cleaning out bowl.
- Whisk for beating eggs, blending liquid ingredients and combining dry ingredients.
- Ice cream scoop or large metal spoon for filling muffin cups.
- Enough muffin tins for at least 12 average muffins.
- Wire rack for cooling muffins.

Maple Ragamuffins

Dark maple syrup gives these easy muffins that deep-down maple flavor. We've added a dash of maple extract for good measure.

1-1/2 cups	all-purpose flour	375 mL
1-1/2 cups	whole wheat flour	375 mL
1 cup	pecan pieces, toasted (see box, p. 28)	250 mL
1 tbsp	baking powder	15 mL
1/2 tsp	salt	2 mL
3/4 cup	plain yogurt	175 mL
3/4 cup	dark maple syrup	175 mL
1/3 cup	butter, melted	75 mL
2	eggs	2
1/2 tsp	maple extract	2 mL
	GARNISH	
12	whole pecans	12
2 tsp	maple syrup	10 mL

- In large bowl, combine all-purpose and whole wheat flours, pecans, baking powder and salt. Whisk together yogurt, maple syrup, butter, eggs and maple extract; pour over dry ingredients. Stir together just until moistened. Spoon into greased or paper-lined muffin cups.
- GARNISH: Place whole pecan on top of each muffin. Bake in 400°F (200°C) oven for 20 minutes or until tops are firm to the touch. Let cool in pan on rack for 3 minutes. Remove muffins from pan to rack; brush with maple syrup. Makes 12 muffins.

Mandarin Muffins

Out West, mandarins are the preferred easy-peeling citrus fruit. In Eastern Canada, seedless sweet clementines from Morocco and Spain get the nod. For either, one 10-ounce (284 mL) can of well-drained mandarin oranges can replace the fresh in these spicy muffins.

1-1/2 cups	all-purpose flour	375 mL
1/2 cup	granulated sugar	125 mL
2-1/2 tsp	baking powder	12 mL
1/2 tsp	nutmeg	2 mL
1/4 tsp	allspice	1 mL
1/4 tsp	salt	1 mL
1	egg	1
3/4 cup	milk	175 mL
1/3 cup	butter, melted	75 mL
1 cup	mandarin orange segments, quartered	250 mL
	TOPPING	
2 tbsp	granulated sugar	25 mL
1 tbsp	grated orange rind	15 mL

- In large bowl, combine flour, sugar, baking powder, nutmeg, allspice and salt. Whisk together egg, milk and butter; pour over dry ingredients. Sprinkle with oranges; stir just until dry ingredients are moistened. Spoon into greased or paper-lined muffin cups, filling three-quarters full.
- TOPPING: Combine sugar with orange rind; sprinkle over batter. Bake in 400°F (200°C) oven for 20 minutes or until tops are firm to the touch. Makes 12 muffins.

Cranberry Oat Muffins ▼

3/4 cup	rolled oats	175 mL
1-1/2 cups	all-purpose flour	375 mL
1 cup	granulated sugar	250 mL
2 tsp	baking powder	10 mL
1/2 tsp	salt	2 mL
1/2 cup	butter	125 mL
2/3 cup	milk	150 mL
1	egg	1
2 cups	coarsely chopped cranberries	500 mL
4 tsp	grated lemon rind	20 mL
	TOPPING	
4 tsp	granulated sugar	20 mL
1 tsp	cinnamon	5 mL

● In food processor or blender, grind rolled oats until powdered; transfer to large bowl. Stir in flour, sugar, baking powder and salt; cut in butter until crumbly.

● Whisk together milk and egg; pour over dry ingredients. Sprinkle with cranberries and lemon rind; stir just until dry ingredients are moistened. Spoon into large greased or paper-lined muffin cups, filling three-quarters full.

● TOPPING: Combine sugar and cinnamon; sprinkle over batter. Bake in 400°F (200°C) oven for 25 to 30 minutes or until tops are firm to the touch. Makes 10 large muffins.

Served warm from the oven, these cranberry-speckled muffins are moist and colorful with a cinnamon sprinkle topping.

Cranberry Coconut Muffins

Cranberries freeze exceptionally well. Just pop a few bags in the freezer as is and you can dip into the berry stash when there's nary a cranberry in the stores. Chop them still frozen and use in muffins just as you would fresh.

2 cups	all-purpose flour	500 mL
3/4 cup	granulated sugar	175 mL
3/4 cup	sweetened shredded coconut	175 mL
1 tbsp	baking powder	15 mL
1 tsp	baking soda	5 mL
1/4 tsp	each cinnamon and salt	1 mL
1-1/4 cups	buttermilk	300 mL
2	eggs	2
1/4 cup	vegetable oil	50 mL
1 tsp	vanilla	5 mL
1 cup	cranberries, chopped	250 mL

- In large bowl, combine flour, sugar, 1/2 cup (125 mL) of the coconut, baking powder, baking soda, cinnamon and salt. Whisk together buttermilk, eggs, oil and vanilla; pour over dry ingredients. Sprinkle with cranberries; stir just until dry ingredients are moistened.
- Spoon into greased or paper-lined muffin cups, filling three-quarters full; sprinkle with remaining coconut. Bake in 400°F (200°C) oven for about 20 minutes or until golden and tops are firm to the touch. Makes 18 muffins.

Light Cranberry Orange Muffins

The amount of fat has been reduced in these refreshing orange-laced muffins.

2 cups	all-purpose flour	500 mL
3/4 cup	granulated sugar	175 mL
2 tsp	baking powder	10 mL
1 tsp	baking soda	5 mL
1/4 tsp	cinnamon	1 mL
1-1/4 cups	chopped cranberries	300 mL
1/2 cup	grated peeled apple	125 mL
1 cup	orange juice	250 mL
1	egg	1
1	egg white	1
2 tbsp	butter, melted	25 mL
1-1/2 tsp	vanilla	7 mL

- In large bowl, combine flour, sugar, baking powder, baking soda and cinnamon; stir in 1 cup (250 mL) of the cranberries and apple. Whisk together orange juice, egg, egg white, butter and vanilla; pour over dry ingredients. Stir together just until moistened.
- Spoon into greased or paper-lined muffin cups; sprinkle with remaining cranberries. Bake in 350°F (180°C) oven for 20 to 25 minutes or until golden and tops are firm to the touch. Makes 12 muffins.

FOR PERFECT MUFFINS EVERY TIME

1. Read the recipe through, assemble your equipment and measure out ingredients.
2. Grease muffin tins well using shortening or vegetable oil spray, or line with paper muffin cups.
3. Adjust oven rack to the middle of the oven and preheat the oven.
4. Easy does it! Mixing muffins requires just a few strokes to blend the liquid ingredients into the dry. As soon as you see the dry disappear, even if a few lumps remain, you're ready to scoop the batter.
5. Fill the muffin cups anywhere from two-thirds or three-quarters full to right up to the top. The more batter in the muffin cups, the bigger the muffin. Check individual recipes for specific instructions.
6. A well-done muffin has an attractive rounded top that's firm to the touch, golden, golden brown or gloriously brown, depending on the ingredients. When a tester inserted in the center of the muffin comes out clean, the muffin is done.
7. Let muffins sit in their tins for 5 minutes to firm up slightly before transferring to rack to cool, or to serviette-lined basket to whisk to the table.

Apple Pie Muffins ▲

2-1/4 cups	all-purpose flour	550 mL
1-1/2 cups	packed brown sugar	375 mL
1 tsp	baking soda	5 mL
1/2 tsp	salt	2 mL
1	egg	1
1 cup	buttermilk	250 mL
1/2 cup	butter, melted	125 mL
1 tsp	vanilla	5 mL
2 cups	diced peeled apples	500 mL
	TOPPING	
1/2 cup	packed brown sugar	125 mL
1/2 cup	chopped pecans	125 mL
1/3 cup	all-purpose flour	75 mL
1 tsp	cinnamon	5 mL
2 tbsp	butter, melted	25 mL

● TOPPING: In bowl, stir together brown sugar, pecans, flour and cinnamon. Drizzle with butter, tossing with fork. Set aside.

● In large bowl, combine flour, sugar, baking soda and salt. Whisk together egg, buttermilk, butter and vanilla; pour over dry ingredients. Sprinkle with apples; stir just until dry ingredients are moistened.

● Spoon into large greased or paper-lined muffin cups; sprinkle with topping. Bake in 375°F (190°C) oven for about 25 minutes or until tops are firm to the touch. Makes 16 muffins.

When Canadian Living Test Kitchen manager Daphna Rabinovitch was pastry chef at Toronto's David Wood Food Shop, these crusty-topped, apple-filled muffins (featured on the front cover) were one of her best-sellers. They're ideal for a brunch party.

NO BUTTERMILK?

Buttermilk, which goes hand in hand with baking soda to produce a high, light muffin, is not always in your fridge. To substitute, pour 1 tbsp (15 mL) white vinegar into a measuring cup and pour in enough milk to make 1 cup (250 mL). Stir and let stand for 5 to 10 minutes and use as buttermilk.

Peanut and Banana Muffins

A rich banana-flavored muffin with the crunch of peanuts makes a nice treat in a packed lunch. The banana slice on top is a hint of the tropical fruitiness in each delicious bite.

1-1/2 cups	all-purpose flour	375 mL
1/2 cup	whole wheat flour	125 mL
1/2 cup	chopped unsalted peanuts	125 mL
1/3 cup	packed brown sugar	75 mL
2 tsp	baking powder	10 mL
1 tsp	baking soda	5 mL
1/2 tsp	salt	2 mL
1/4 tsp	nutmeg	1 mL
1	egg	1
2 cups	mashed bananas (about 6)	500 mL
1/2 cup	plain yogurt	125 mL
1/4 cup	butter, melted	50 mL
1 tsp	vanilla	5 mL
12	banana slices	12

● In large bowl, combine all-purpose and whole wheat flours, peanuts, sugar, baking powder, baking soda, salt and nutmeg. In separate bowl, beat egg; whisk in bananas, yogurt, butter and vanilla. Pour over dry ingredients; stir together just until moistened.

● Spoon into greased or paper-lined muffin cups; top each muffin with banana slice. Bake in 350°F (180°C) oven for about 25 minutes or until tops are firm to the touch. Makes 12 muffins.

Pumpkin, Orange and Raisin Muffins

The annual Pumpkinfest in Port Elgin, Ontario, celebrates pumpkins and superlative home baking. This prizewinning muffin is equally delicious made with your own pumpkin or the canned variety.

2 cups	all-purpose flour	500 mL
1 cup	raisins	250 mL
1/3 cup	packed brown sugar	75 mL
1-1/2 tsp	baking powder	7 mL
1 tsp	baking soda	5 mL
1/2 tsp	each salt, cinnamon, ginger and nutmeg	2 mL
1	egg	1
1-3/4 cups	pumpkin purée	425 mL
1/3 cup	vegetable oil	75 mL
2 tbsp	coarsely grated orange rind	25 mL
1/2 cup	orange juice	125 mL

● In large bowl, combine flour, raisins, sugar, baking powder, baking soda, salt, cinnamon, ginger and nutmeg. In separate bowl, beat egg; blend in pumpkin, oil, orange rind and juice. Pour over dry ingredients; stir together just until moistened.

● Spoon into large greased or paper-lined muffin cups, filling to top. Bake in 375°F (190°C) oven for about 25 minutes or until golden and tops are firm to the touch. Makes 12 muffins.

FREEZING MUFFINS

● Let muffins cool completely before freezing.

● For best results, wrap each muffin in plastic wrap and enclose batch of wrapped muffins in airtight container or freezer bag. The wrapping helps to keep the muffins fresher, and makes popping a muffin into a lunch bag or take-along breakfast a breeze.

● Freeze for up to two weeks.

● Thaw muffins at room temperature while still wrapped, or heat in microwave at High for 30 to 60 seconds. Unwrap muffin before microwaving and wrap lightly in paper towel.

STOCKING UP FOR MUFFINS

Keep your baking cupboard and refrigerator well stocked with the following ingredients so that making muffins can be a spur-of-the-moment project or part of your weekly routine.

- all-purpose and whole wheat flours
- natural bran
- rolled oats and cornmeal
- applesauce
- brown and granulated sugars
- vegetable oil
- baking powder and baking soda
- salt
- peanut butter
- cinnamon, ginger and nutmeg
- molasses and honey
- coconut, nuts and dried fruit such as raisins, dates, prunes, figs and apricots
- eggs, butter, milk, buttermilk and yogurt
- carrots, oranges and lemons

New Marigold Muffins

2 cups	all-purpose flour	500 mL
1 cup	raisins	250 mL
3/4 cup	packed brown sugar	175 mL
2/3 cup	shredded coconut	150 mL
4 tsp	cinnamon	20 mL
2 tsp	baking soda	10 mL
3/4 tsp	salt	4 mL
3	eggs	3
2/3 cup	plain yogurt	150 mL
1/3 cup	vegetable oil	75 mL
2 tsp	vanilla	10 mL
3 cups	grated carrots	750 mL
1 cup	grated peeled apple	250 mL

- In large bowl, combine flour, raisins, sugar, coconut, cinnamon, baking soda and salt. In separate bowl, whisk together eggs, yogurt, oil and vanilla; stir in carrots and apple. Pour over dry ingredients; stir together just until moistened.
- Spoon into greased or paper-lined muffin cups. Bake in 350°F (180°C) oven for 30 to 35 minutes or until tops are firm to the touch. Makes 18 muffins.

Here's a lighter, freezer-friendly version of the ever-popular carrot, apple and raisin muffin. Pack it along with a banana and container of yogurt for a healthy and tasty totable breakfast.

Rhubarb Muffins

2-1/2 cups	all-purpose flour	625 mL
1 tsp	baking soda	5 mL
1/2 tsp	salt	2 mL
1-1/4 cups	packed brown sugar	300 mL
1/2 cup	vegetable oil	125 mL
1	egg	1
1 cup	buttermilk	250 mL
1 tsp	vanilla	5 mL
2 cups	chopped rhubarb	500 mL
	TOPPING	
1/2 cup	packed brown sugar	125 mL
1 tbsp	butter, melted	15 mL
1/2 tsp	cinnamon	2 mL

- In large bowl, combine flour, baking soda and salt. In separate bowl, whisk together sugar and oil; whisk in egg, buttermilk and vanilla. Pour over dry ingredients; sprinkle with rhubarb and stir just until dry ingredients are moistened. Spoon into greased or paper-lined muffin cups, filling three-quarters full.
- TOPPING: Combine sugar, butter and cinnamon; sprinkle over batter. Bake in 350°F (180°C) oven for 20 to 25 minutes or until tops are firm to the touch. Makes 18 muffins.

In the world of baking, nothing signals spring better than rhubarb. A delight in crumbles, crisps and pies, rhubarb also lends tangy snippets to muffins. These are perfect for a spring tea or brunch.

Orange and Pecan Bran Muffins ▲

Bliss is a weekend morning with time to savor a special muffin, a slice of Brie, some fruit — and a leisurely café au lait.

2 cups	natural bran	500 mL
1 cup	all-purpose flour	250 mL
1 cup	chopped dates	250 mL
1/2 cup	chopped pecans	125 mL
1/4 cup	wheat germ	50 mL
1 tbsp	grated orange rind	15 mL
2 tsp	baking soda	10 mL
1/2 tsp	salt	2 mL
1-3/4 cups	buttermilk	425 mL
1/3 cup	butter, melted, or vegetable oil	75 mL
1/3 cup	molasses or corn syrup	75 mL

● In large bowl, combine bran, flour, dates, pecans, wheat germ, orange rind, baking soda and salt. Whisk together buttermilk, butter and molasses; pour over dry ingredients. Stir together just until moistened.

● Spoon into large greased or paper-lined muffin cups, filling to top. Bake in 400°F (200°C) oven for 20 to 25 minutes or until tops are firm to the touch. Makes 12 muffins.

COMBINING DRY INGREDIENTS

Use whisk to make sure that flour, baking powder or baking soda, salt and spices are well combined before adding wet ingredients.

Banana Pineapple Bran Muffins

1 cup	mashed bananas	250 mL
1/2 cup	packed brown sugar	125 mL
1/2 cup	natural bran	125 mL
1/2 cup	unsweetened crushed pineapple	125 mL
1/3 cup	vegetable oil	75 mL
1 tbsp	grated orange rind	15 mL
1-1/2 tsp	vanilla	7 mL
2	eggs	2
1-1/2 cups	all-purpose flour	375 mL
2/3 cup	skim milk powder	150 mL
1-1/2 tsp	baking powder	7 mL
1 tsp	baking soda	5 mL
1/4 tsp	salt	1 mL

● In bowl, combine bananas, sugar, bran, pineapple, oil, orange rind and vanilla; let stand for 5 minutes. Beat in eggs, one at a time.

● In large bowl, combine flour, milk powder, baking powder, baking soda and salt. Pour banana mixture over dry ingredients. Stir together just until moistened.

● Spoon into greased or paper-lined muffin cups. Bake in 400°F (200°C) oven for 18 to 20 minutes or until tops are firm to the touch. Makes 12 muffins.

There's lots of fruit flavor in these satisfying bran muffins. Natural bran, from wheat, is available in bulk stores, health food stores and in the cereal or baking sections of supermarkets. Store in an airtight container in the refrigerator.

Scoop-and-Bake Muffins

4 cups	100% Bran cereal	1 L
2 cups	boiling water	500 mL
5 cups	all-purpose flour	1.25 L
2 cups	natural bran	500 mL
2 cups	raisins	500 mL
5 tsp	baking soda	25 mL
1 tsp	salt	5 mL
2 cups	packed brown sugar	500 mL
1 cup	vegetable oil	250 mL
4	eggs	4
4 cups	buttermilk	1 L

● In bowl, combine cereal and boiling water; let cool.

● In large bowl, combine flour, natural bran, raisins, baking soda and salt. In separate bowl, whisk together sugar, oil and eggs; blend in buttermilk. Pour over dry ingredients; add cereal mixture. Stir together just until moistened. *(Batter can be refrigerated in airtight container for up to 1 week.)*

● Spoon into large greased or paper-lined muffin cups. Bake in 350°F (180°C) oven for about 30 minutes or until tops are firm to the touch. Makes 3-1/2 dozen muffins.

A ready-to-bake big-batch muffin mix is a staple in many Canadian kitchens. This delicious one comes from Flint's Inn, a charming bed-and-breakfast in Stratford, Ontario. For a change of taste, replace the raisins with other dried fruits such as dates or apricots and add a touch of grated orange or lemon rind.

A MUFFIN BREAKFAST

Muffins are so make-ahead, so portable and so easy to eat that they have evolved from a breakfast treat into an everyday breakfast institution. Choose a lower-fat muffin with bran, oats or cereal and add yogurt and fruit to make up three of the four food groups. Or, include a slice of cheese with your muffin and fruit.

Yogurt Bran Muffins ▼

Serve up a basketful of these nutritious muffins for breakfast and get everyone in your household off to a healthy start.

1-1/4 cups	all-purpose flour	300 mL
1-1/4 cups	natural bran	300 mL
3/4 cups	packed brown sugar	175 mL
1 tbsp	baking powder	15 mL
1 tsp	baking soda	5 mL
1/4 tsp	each cinnamon and salt	1 mL
1 cup	chopped dried apricots or dates, or whole raisins	250 mL
1 cup	plain yogurt	250 mL
1/4 cup	vegetable oil	50 mL
1	egg	1
1-1/2 tsp	vanilla	7 mL

● In large bowl, combine flour, bran, sugar, baking powder, baking soda, cinnamon and salt. Reserve 2 tbsp (25 mL) of the apricots; stir remaining apricots into bowl. Whisk together yogurt, oil, egg and vanilla; pour over dry ingredients. Stir together just until moistened.

● Spoon into large greased or paper-lined muffin cups, filling three-quarters full; press reserved apricots into tops. Bake in 375°F (190°C) oven for 20 to 25 minutes or until golden and tops are firm to the touch. Makes 12 muffins.

Spicy Oatmeal Muffins

1-1/2 cups	all-purpose flour	375 mL
1 cup	quick-cooking rolled oats	250 mL
1 cup	raisins	250 mL
1/2 cup	packed brown sugar	125 mL
1 tsp	baking powder	5 mL
1 tsp	baking soda	5 mL
1-1/2 tsp	cinnamon	7 mL
1/2 tsp	nutmeg	2 mL
1	egg	1
1-3/4 cups	unsweetened applesauce	425 mL
1/3 cup	vegetable oil	75 mL
1 tsp	vanilla	5 mL

● In large bowl, combine flour, rolled oats, raisins, sugar, baking powder, baking soda, cinnamon and nutmeg. Whisk together egg, applesauce, oil and vanilla; pour over dry ingredients. Stir together just until moistened.

● Spoon into greased or paper-lined muffin cups, filling three-quarters full. Bake in 375°F (190°C) oven for about 20 minutes or until golden brown and tops are firm to the touch. Makes 12 muffins.

A generous helping of finely puréed applesauce makes these wholesome muffins wonderfully moist and tasty. Add a tangy twist by substituting dried cherries for the raisins.

Raisin Breakfast Bars

2 cups	raisins	500 mL
1 cup	whole wheat flour	250 mL
1 cup	All-Bran cereal	250 mL
2/3 cup	packed brown sugar	150 mL
1/2 cup	all-purpose flour	125 mL
2 tsp	baking soda	10 mL
1/2 tsp	salt	2 mL
2	eggs	2
1-1/2 cups	plain yogurt	375 mL
1/4 cup	vegetable oil	50 mL
1 tsp	vanilla	5 mL
1 tbsp	coarsely grated orange rind	15 mL

● In large bowl, combine raisins, whole wheat flour, cereal, sugar, all-purpose flour, baking soda and salt. Whisk together eggs, yogurt, oil, vanilla and orange rind; pour over dry ingredients. Stir together just until moistened.

● Pour into greased 9-inch (2.5 L) square cake pan. Bake in 350°F (180°C) oven for 25 to 30 minutes or until tester inserted in center comes out clean and cake has come away from sides of pan. Let cool on rack; cut into bars. Makes 16 bars.

They smell like cake and they look like cake, but they're really muffin bars to eat with a piece of fruit and a glass of milk. You can vary the dried fruit to please your household.

Golden Cornsticks or Muffins

1 cup	cornmeal	250 mL
1 cup	shredded old Cheddar cheese	250 mL
1 cup	all-purpose flour	250 mL
2 tbsp	chopped fresh coriander	25 mL
3/4 tsp	salt	4 mL
1/2 tsp	baking soda	2 mL
3	eggs	3
1	can (10 oz/284 mL) creamed corn	1
1 cup	buttermilk	250 mL
1/4 cup	butter, melted	50 mL

● In large bowl, combine cornmeal, Cheddar, flour, coriander, salt and baking soda. Whisk together eggs, corn, buttermilk and butter; pour over dry ingredients. Stir together just until moistened.

● Spoon into greased 5-inch (12 cm) long cornstick moulds or into greased or paper-lined muffin cups. Bake in 400°F (200°C) oven for 25 to 30 minutes or until tops are firm to the touch. Makes 16 cornsticks or 12 muffins.

Creamed corn makes especially fine corn muffins, adding bits of corn and considerable moistness. Serve with chili, baked beans or stews.

Canadian Living's Best Muffin Mix

There's more than one way to make a muffin, and a homemade mix featuring bran and whole wheat flour is one of the smartest. Keep the recipes handy with the mix so that the pleasure of baking muffins can be shared around the household. With a handy mix, it's just minutes before fresh muffins are ready for breakfasts and lunch-bag treats.

5-1/2 cups	all-purpose flour	1.375 L
2-1/4 cups	whole wheat flour	550 mL
2-1/4 cups	natural bran	550 mL
1-3/4 cups	skim milk powder	425 mL
1-1/2 cups	granulated sugar	375 mL
2 tbsp	baking powder	25 mL
2 tsp	salt	10 mL

● In large bowl, stir together all-purpose and whole wheat flours, bran, milk powder, sugar, baking powder and salt until combined. Transfer to airtight container; store in cool, dry place. Stir well before using. Makes about 12 cups (3 L).

*An array of muffins and fresh fruit is inspiration for a leisurely brunch.
Toppings such as apple butter, low-sugar jams and drained yogurt cheese add to the pleasure.*

Apple Carrot Muffins

2-3/4 cups	Best Muffin Mix	675 mL
1-1/2 cups	shredded carrots (about 5 small)	375 mL
2/3 cup	raisins	150 mL
1 tsp	cinnamon	5 mL
1 tsp	nutmeg	5 mL
1/2 tsp	baking soda	2 mL
3/4 cup	apple juice	175 mL
1/3 cup	vegetable oil	75 mL
1/4 cup	fancy molasses	50 mL
1	egg	1
1 tsp	vanilla	5 mL

- In large bowl, stir together Best Muffin Mix, carrots, raisins, cinnamon, nutmeg and baking soda. Whisk together apple juice, oil, molasses, egg and vanilla; pour over dry ingredients. Stir together just until moistened.
- Spoon into greased or paper-lined muffin cups. Bake in 375°F (190°C) oven for about 30 minutes or until tops are firm to the touch. Makes 9 muffins.

With carrots in most crispers, this is the kind of muffin you can mix up anytime without a special trip to the store.

Healthy-Start Muffins

1 cup	All-Bran cereal	250 mL
1-1/4 cups	water	300 mL
1/3 cup	vegetable oil	75 mL
1/4 cup	fancy molasses	50 mL
1	egg	1
1 tsp	vanilla	5 mL
2-3/4 cups	Best Muffin Mix	675 mL
3/4 cup	chopped prunes	175 mL
1/3 cup	green pumpkin seeds	75 mL
2 tsp	cinnamon	10 mL
1/2 tsp	baking soda	2 mL

- In bowl, soak cereal in water for 5 minutes or until softened; whisk in oil, molasses, egg and vanilla.
- In large bowl, stir together Best Muffin Mix, prunes, pumpkin seeds, cinnamon and baking soda. Pour cereal mixture over dry ingredients; stir together just until moistened.
- Spoon into greased or paper-lined muffin cups. Bake in 375°F (190°C) oven for about 30 minutes or until tops are firm to the touch. Makes 9 muffins.

Pack in bran in the form of cereal, add prunes for sweetness and fiber, then sprinkle in green pumpkin seeds for color and crunch — and you're on your way to a great day.

Chocolate Banana Muffins

2-3/4 cups	Best Muffin Mix	675 mL
3/4 cup	chocolate chips	175 mL
1 cup	mashed bananas (about 3 small)	250 mL
1/3 cup	water	75 mL
1/3 cup	vegetable oil	75 mL
1	egg	1
1 tsp	vanilla	5 mL
9	thin banana slices	9

- In large bowl, stir Best Muffin Mix with chocolate chips. Whisk together banana, water, oil, egg and vanilla; pour over dry ingredients. Stir together just until moistened.
- Spoon into greased or paper-lined muffin cups; top each with banana slice. Bake in 375°F (190°C) oven for about 30 minutes or until tops are firm to the touch. Makes 9 muffins.

These utterly delicious, moist muffins deliver special-occasion flavor any time you make them.

Jumbo Arizona Muffins

Big and bold with Tex-Mex flavors, these muffins are perfect partners with lunchtime or supper soups and salads, or with chili or baked ham.

1-1/2 cups	all-purpose flour	375 mL
1-1/2 cups	cornmeal	375 mL
1 cup	corn kernels	250 mL
2 tbsp	granulated sugar	25 mL
2 tbsp	baking powder	25 mL
2 tbsp	finely chopped jalapeño pepper	25 mL
1	large sweet red pepper, diced	1
3/4 tsp	salt	4 mL
1/4 tsp	cayenne pepper (optional)	1 mL
3	eggs	3
1-1/2 cups	milk	375 mL
1/2 cup	butter, melted	125 mL
1-1/2 cups	shredded mozzarella cheese	375 mL

● In large bowl, combine flour, cornmeal, corn, sugar, baking powder, jalapeño pepper, red pepper, salt, and cayenne pepper (if using). Whisk together eggs, milk and butter; pour over dry ingredients. Stir together just until moistened.

● Spoon enough of the batter into nine 3/4-cup (175 mL) greased custard cups to fill halfway to top. Form cheese into 9 balls; lightly press each into center of batter. Spoon remaining batter over top. Bake in 400°F (200°C) oven for 25 to 30 minutes or until golden and tops are firm to the touch. Makes 9 large muffins.

TIP: You can use fresh or frozen corn or drained canned kernels. Similarly, the jalapeño pepper can be canned or fresh, depending on availability.

Surprise Cornmeal Muffins

Bite into one of these golden muffins, and you'll find a surprise filling you can vary to suit everyone's tastes. Choose blueberries, peanut butter, cream cheese, jam, raisins, a prune, apple butter — whatever appeals or is close at hand.

1-1/4 cups	cake-and-pastry flour	300 mL
1 cup	cornmeal	250 mL
2 tsp	baking powder	10 mL
1 tsp	baking soda	5 mL
1/2 tsp	salt	2 mL
1/2 cup	shortening	125 mL
1/2 cup	granulated sugar	125 mL
1	egg	1
1 cup	milk	250 mL
1/2 cup	plain yogurt	125 mL
1/4 cup	filling	50 mL

● In large bowl, combine flour, cornmeal, baking powder, baking soda and salt. In separate bowl, beat shortening with sugar until fluffy; beat in egg, milk and yogurt. Stir into dry ingredients just until moistened.

● Spoon half of the batter into greased or paper-lined muffin cups, filling halfway to top. Spoon 1 tsp (5 mL) filling over each; top with remaining batter. Bake in 400°F (200°C) oven for 20 to 25 minutes or until tops are firm to the touch. Makes 12 muffins.

STORING MUFFINS

● Most muffins, except those containing meat or fish, keep fresh stored in an airtight container at room temperature for up to 2 days. Refrigerate any muffins containing meat or fish.

● Reheat muffins, lightly wrapped in paper towel, at High in the microwave for about 20 seconds, or split and warm in toaster oven.

Salmon Muffins

1-1/2 cups	all-purpose flour	375 mL
1/4 cup	shredded old Cheddar cheese	50 mL
1 tbsp	granulated sugar	15 mL
2 tsp	baking powder	10 mL
1/2 tsp	salt	2 mL
1	can (7-1/2 oz/213 g) sockeye salmon	1
1/3 cup	sour cream	75 mL
1/4 cup	finely chopped celery	50 mL
1/4 cup	chopped green onion	50 mL
1 tbsp	chopped fresh dill	15 mL
1/4 tsp	pepper	1 mL
1	egg	1
3/4 cup	milk	175 mL
1/3 cup	vegetable oil	75 mL

● In large bowl, combine flour, Cheddar, sugar, baking powder and salt.

● Drain salmon; discard skin. In separate bowl, crush bones into salmon; stir in sour cream, celery, green onion, dill and pepper.

● Whisk together egg, milk and oil; pour over dry ingredients. Pour salmon mixture over top; stir just until dry ingredients are moistened.

● Spoon into greased or paper-lined muffin cups. Bake in 375°F (190°C) oven for 20 to 25 minutes or until golden brown and tops are firm to the touch. Makes 10 muffins.

VARIATION

● SMOKED SALMON MUFFINETTES: ▲ Substitute 3/4 cup (175 mL) chopped smoked salmon for canned salmon; bake in greased mini muffin cups for about 20 minutes or until tops are firm to the touch. Makes 24 muffins.

TIP: The mini version (photo above) makes a pretty appetizer. Just cut out a little cone from each muffin top; fill hollow with sour cream, top with a dill sprig and replace cone.

These savory salmon muffins are a novel — and very packable! — version of a salmon sandwich. At home, serve with a salad or soup for a light supper or weekend lunch.

Pizza Muffins

You can substitute chopped sweet red pepper for the sun-dried tomatoes, omitting the soaking step. These great-looking, great-tasting muffins are perfect for packed lunches.

1/3 cup	sun-dried tomatoes	75 mL
1-1/2 cups	all-purpose flour	375 mL
1/3 cup	freshly grated Parmesan cheese	75 mL
1 tbsp	granulated sugar	15 mL
2 tsp	baking powder	10 mL
2 tsp	dried oregano	10 mL
1/2 tsp	salt	2 mL
1/4 tsp	pepper	1 mL
3/4 cup	milk	175 mL
1/3 cup	olive oil	75 mL
1	egg	1
8	thin slices pepperoni or tomato	8
1/4 cup	sliced sweet green pepper	50 mL
1/4 cup	shredded mozzarella cheese	50 mL

- Cover tomatoes with boiling water; let stand for 10 minutes or until softened. Drain and dice.
- In large bowl, combine flour, Parmesan, sun-dried tomatoes, sugar, baking powder, oregano, salt and pepper. Whisk together milk, oil and egg; pour over dry ingredients. Stir together just until moistened.
- Spoon into greased or paper-lined muffin cups. Evenly top with pepperoni, green pepper and mozzarella. Bake in 375°F (180°C) oven for 20 to 25 minutes or until tops are firm to the touch. Makes 8 muffins.

Bacon and Green Onion Muffins

These moist, savory muffins are chock-full of the hash-brown breakfast flavor of potatoes, onion and bacon. Any smoked meat such as ham, turkey or chicken can replace the bacon.

1-1/2 cups	all-purpose flour	375 mL
1 tbsp	granulated sugar	15 mL
2 tsp	baking powder	10 mL
1 tsp	pepper	5 mL
1/2 tsp	salt	2 mL
1/2 cup	shredded peeled potato	125 mL
1/2 cup	chopped green onion	125 mL
1/2 cup	chopped cooked drained bacon	125 mL
1/2 cup	milk	125 mL
1/3 cup	vegetable oil	75 mL
1/4 cup	sour cream	50 mL
1	egg	1

	GLAZE	
1 tbsp	milk	15 mL

- In large bowl, combine flour, sugar, baking powder, pepper and salt; stir in potato, onion and bacon. Whisk together milk, oil, sour cream and egg; pour over dry ingredients. Stir together just until moistened. Spoon into greased or paper-lined muffin cups.
- GLAZE: Brush milk over batter. Bake in 375°F (190°C) oven for 20 to 25 minutes or until tops are firm to the touch. Makes 8 muffins.

MUFFIN SIZES

Smaller muffins are perfect for small appetites and school lunches. Our bigger muffins are closer to the giant ones sold in coffee shops and make a more satisfying contribution to an adult breakfast. If you like tinier muffins, look for mini muffin pans designed to allow the smaller quantity of batter to rise into an attractive muffin shape. Remember to use the correct size of paper muffin cup to suit the pan.

Tuna Salad Muffins ▲

1-1/2 cups	all-purpose flour	375 mL
1 tbsp	granulated sugar	15 mL
2 tsp	baking powder	10 mL
1/2 tsp	salt	2 mL
1	can (6-1/2 oz/184 g) tuna	1
1/2 cup	plain yogurt	125 mL
1/4 cup	diced celery	50 mL
1/4 cup	chopped green onion	50 mL
1/4 cup	sliced pimiento-stuffed olives	50 mL
2 tbsp	chopped sweet red pepper	25 mL
1	egg	1
3/4 cup	milk	175 mL
1/3 cup	vegetable oil	75 mL

● In large bowl, combine flour, sugar, baking powder and salt.

● Drain and flake tuna. In separate bowl, combine tuna, yogurt, celery, green onion, olives and red pepper. Whisk together egg, milk and oil; pour over dry ingredients. Pour tuna mixture over top; stir just until dry ingredients are moistened.

● Spoon into large greased or paper-lined muffin cups. Bake in 375°F (190°C) oven for 20 to 25 minutes or until golden brown and tops are firm to the touch. Makes 8 muffins.

Delight the lunchtime crowd with this crunchy and colorful variation on the ever-popular tuna sandwich.

Easy Quick Breads

A generous slice of a moist, fruit-filled loaf is the perfect companion to a relaxing cup of afternoon tea or coffee. All our loaves wrap well for carrying to picnics and potlucks, too.

Lemon Poppy Seed Loaf ▶

With a tangy lemon syrup that seeps addictively into the cake, this ever-popular loaf is a must for teas, snacks and lunches.

1/2 cup	butter, softened	125 mL
1 cup	granulated sugar	250 mL
2	eggs	2
1-1/2 cups	all-purpose flour	375 mL
3 tbsp	poppy seeds	50 mL
1 tbsp	grated lemon rind	15 mL
1 tsp	baking powder	5 mL
1/4 tsp	salt	1 mL
1/2 cup	milk	125 mL
	LEMON SYRUP	
1/3 cup	granulated sugar	75 mL
1 tsp	grated lemon rind	5 mL
1/3 cup	lemon juice	75 mL

- In large bowl, beat butter with sugar until fluffy; beat in eggs, one at a time.
- In separate bowl, combine flour, poppy seeds, lemon rind, baking powder and salt; stir into butter mixture alternately with milk, making three additions of dry and two of milk.
- Pour into greased 8- x 4-inch (1.5 L) loaf pan. Bake in 325°F (160°C) oven for about 1 hour or until tester inserted in center comes out clean. Place pan on rack.
- LEMON SYRUP: In microwaveable measure or in saucepan on stove, warm sugar, lemon rind and juice until sugar dissolves. With skewer, pierce hot loaf in 12 places right to bottom; pour lemon syrup over loaf. Let cool in pan for 30 minutes; turn out onto rack and let cool completely. Wrap and let stand overnight before slicing. Makes 1 loaf.

Crunchy Banana Bread

This light-in-fat loaf has lots of deep-down banana flavor plus a unique crunchy texture, thanks to millet (available in bulk and health food stores).

1/2 cup	milk	125 mL
1-1/2 tsp	white vinegar	7 mL
3/4 cup	packed brown sugar	175 mL
1 tbsp	butter, softened	15 mL
1 cup	mashed bananas	250 mL
2	eggs	2
1 cup	graham flour	250 mL
1 cup	all-purpose flour	250 mL
1 tsp	baking powder	5 mL
1 tsp	baking soda	5 mL
1/4 tsp	salt	1 mL
1/3 cup	millet	75 mL

- Combine milk and vinegar; set aside.
- In large bowl, beat sugar with butter; beat in bananas and eggs. Combine graham and all-purpose flours, baking powder, baking soda and salt; stir into banana mixture alternately with milk mixture, making three additions of dry and two of milk. Stir in millet.
- Pour into well-greased 9- x 5-inch (2 L) loaf pan. Bake in 350°F (180°C) oven for 45 to 50 minutes or until tester inserted in center comes out clean. Makes 1 loaf.

Blueberry Lemon Loaf

Canadian baking and blueberries — together again in a reputation-making streusel-topped loaf. This one's so rich-tasting and satisfying, you won't need to butter the slices.

1/2 cup	butter, softened	125 mL
1 cup	packed brown sugar	250 mL
2	eggs	2
2 tbsp	lemon juice	25 mL
1-1/2 tsp	vanilla	7 mL
2 cups	all-purpose flour	500 mL
1 tbsp	grated lemon rind	15 mL
2 tsp	baking powder	10 mL
1/4 tsp	each salt and cinnamon	1 mL
1/2 cup	milk	125 mL
1-1/2 cups	blueberries (fresh or frozen)	375 mL
	TOPPING	
1/4 cup	all-purpose flour	50 mL
2 tbsp	granulated sugar	25 mL
2 tbsp	packed brown sugar	25 mL
1/4 tsp	cinnamon	1 mL
2 tbsp	butter	25 mL

● TOPPING: In bowl, combine flour, granulated and brown sugars and cinnamon. With pastry blender or two knives, cut in butter until in fine crumbs. Set aside.

● In large bowl, beat butter with sugar until fluffy; beat in eggs, one at a time. Beat in lemon juice and vanilla.

● Combine flour, lemon rind, baking powder, salt and cinnamon; stir into butter mixture alternately with milk, making three additions of dry and two of milk. Gently fold in half of the blueberries.

● Pour into greased 8- x 4-inch (1.5 L) loaf pan; sprinkle with remaining blueberries. Sprinkle with topping. Bake in 350°F (180°C) oven for about 1 hour or until tester inserted in center comes out clean. Makes 1 loaf.

Pistachio Apricot Tea Bread ▸

Natural-colored pistachios — in tan shells rather than the red of the dyed snacking variety — are the basis of an elegant loaf. Pistachios, available in many bulk food stores and nut shops, are easy to shell. In a pinch, substitute almonds or hazelnuts.

1/2 cup	unsalted butter	125 mL
3/4 cup	granulated sugar	175 mL
2	eggs	2
1 tbsp	grated lemon rind	15 mL
1/2 tsp	almond extract	2 mL
2 cups	all-purpose flour	500 mL
2 tsp	baking powder	10 mL
1 tsp	baking soda	5 mL
3/4 cup	buttermilk or plain yogurt	175 mL
3/4 cup	dried apricots, diced	175 mL
1/2 cup	finely chopped pistachio nuts, toasted	125 mL

● In large bowl, beat butter with sugar until fluffy. Beat in eggs, one at a time. Beat in lemon rind and almond extract.

● Combine flour, baking powder and baking soda; stir into butter mixture alternately with buttermilk, making three additions of dry and two of buttermilk. Fold in apricots and pistachios.

● Pour into waxed paper-lined 9- x 5-inch (2 L) loaf pan. Bake in 350°F (180°C) oven for about 1 hour or until tester inserted in center comes out clean. Makes 1 loaf.

TOASTING NUTS

Spread nuts on baking sheet and bake in 350°F (180°C) oven for 5 to 10 minutes. Or, spread on microwaveable plate and microwave on High for 6 to 8 minutes, rearranging underbrowned ones to the edge of the plate and browned ones to the center. For smaller amounts, use a toaster oven or a dry skillet over medium heat, tossing nuts occasionally. For hazelnuts, transfer to clean tea towel and rub off skins.

Pumpkin, Date and Nut Loaf

From the annual Pumpkinfest baking contest in Port Elgin, Ontario, comes this winner of a rich, moist pumpkin loaf. A slice, spread with cream cheese, makes a delicious breakfast, quick lunch or indulgent snack.

1	pkg (4 oz/125 g) cream cheese	1
1/4 cup	butter, softened	50 mL
1-1/4 cups	packed brown sugar	300 mL
2	eggs	2
1 tsp	vanilla	5 mL
1-3/4 cups	all-purpose flour	425 mL
1 tsp	baking soda	5 mL
1/2 tsp	baking powder	2 mL
1/2 tsp	salt	2 mL
1/2 tsp	cinnamon	2 mL
1/4 tsp	nutmeg	1 mL
2/3 cup	chopped dates	150 mL
2/3 cup	chopped pecans, toasted (see box, p. 28)	150 mL
1 cup	pumpkin purée	250 mL

● In large bowl, beat together cream cheese, butter and sugar until fluffy. Beat in eggs, one at a time; beat in vanilla.

● In separate bowl, combine flour, baking soda, baking powder, salt, cinnamon and nutmeg; stir in dates and pecans. Stir half into cheese mixture; mix in pumpkin, then remaining flour mixture.

● Spread in greased 9- x 5-inch (2 L) loaf pan. Bake in 350°F (180°C) oven for about 50 minutes or until tester inserted in center comes out clean. Let cool in pan for 15 minutes; turn out onto rack and let cool completely. Wrap and store for 1 day before slicing. Makes 1 loaf.

Tropical Banana Bread

A shredded coconut topping adds a delicious touch to a banana raisin loaf.

1/2 cup	butter, softened	125 mL
1 cup	packed brown sugar	250 mL
3	eggs	3
1 tsp	vanilla	5 mL
2 cups	all-purpose flour	500 mL
1 tsp	baking powder	5 mL
1 tsp	baking soda	5 mL
1/2 tsp	cinnamon	2 mL
1 cup	mashed bananas	250 mL
1 cup	raisins	250 mL

	TOPPING	
1/2 cup	shredded coconut	125 mL
1/4 cup	packed brown sugar	50 mL
1 tbsp	butter, softened	15 mL
1-1/2 tsp	all-purpose flour	7 mL
1/4 tsp	cinnamon	1 mL

● TOPPING: In small bowl, combine coconut, sugar, butter, flour and cinnamon until crumbly; set aside.

● In large bowl, beat butter with sugar until fluffy; beat in eggs, one at a time, beating well after each addition. Stir in vanilla.

● Combine flour, baking powder, baking soda and cinnamon; stir into butter mixture alternately with bananas, making three additions of flour mixture and two of bananas. Fold in raisins.

● Pour into greased 9- x 5-inch (2 L) loaf pan; sprinkle with topping. Bake in 325°F (160°C) oven for about 1 hour or until tester inserted in center comes out clean and loaf is firm. Makes 1 loaf.

BANANAS FOR BAKING

● Bananas for baking must be ripe. Plan to make banana bread and muffins when the fruit is perfumed and golden with deep-brown freckles. The bananas can even be brown as long as they are not bruised.

● When an oversupply of ripe bargain bananas looms in your fruitbowl, freeze them as is and bring them out to thaw, peel and include in baking when the yearning for a good banana bread or muffins hits.

● Three medium to large bananas are needed to make 1 cup (250 mL) mashed bananas. Use a fork or potato masher to mash the fruit.

QUICK-BREAD BASICS

Pan Preparation

- A well-greased loaf pan is often not quite good enough to get a hot and still fragile loaf out of the pan in one piece. For a guaranteed clean exit from pan, line greased pan with waxed or parchment paper cut to fit. You don't need to grease this paper, but be sure to peel it off before slicing the loaf.

Mixing

- Some loaves follow the muffin method — quick, deft strokes incorporating liquid ingredients into the dry. Others are more like cakes, with butter and sugar beaten until fluffy and creamy before beating in eggs, then adding dry and liquid ingredients.

Baking

- Don't worry if your loaves rise up and crack along the length of the loaf. That's typical of loaves.
- To test a loaf for doneness, watch for a golden brown crust that's firm to the touch. The loaf will come away from the sides of the pan as it finishes baking and it will have a toasty baked fragrance.
- Insert a cake tester or skewer into the center of the loaf. If the tester comes out gummy or wet, the loaf needs more baking time.

Cooling

- Let loaves cool for about 15 minutes in pan before turning them out to cool, right side up, on rack.
- Let loaves cool completely before wrapping in foil and storing, preferably in airtight container. Most loaves cut better and are tastier if allowed to mellow one day before slicing.

Freezing

- To freeze, wrap loaf well in plastic wrap or foil before enclosing in airtight container. If planning to use the whole loaf, freeze whole for up to one month. Or, build flexibility into your freezer contents — cut loaf in half to have something delicious to serve on more than one occasion, or cut and wrap individual slices in plastic wrap before enclosing in airtight container.

Strawberry Tea Bread

A berry in every bite! What more could a strawberry lover need or want?

3 cups	strawberries, coarsely chopped	750 mL
1 cup	chopped almonds	250 mL
3-1/2 cups	all-purpose flour	875 mL
1 cup	butter, softened	250 mL
1-1/2 cups	granulated sugar	375 mL
3	eggs	3
1/2 tsp	almond extract	2 mL
2 tsp	baking powder	10 mL
3/4 tsp	baking soda	4 mL
3/4 tsp	salt	4 mL
1/2 tsp	cinnamon	2 mL
1/4 tsp	nutmeg	1 mL
3/4 cup	buttermilk	175 mL

- In bowl, gently toss together strawberries, almonds and 1/4 cup (50 mL) of the flour; set aside.
- In large bowl, beat butter with sugar until fluffy; beat in eggs, one at a time. Beat in almond extract.
- Combine remaining flour, baking powder, baking soda, salt, cinnamon and nutmeg; stir into butter mixture alternately with buttermilk, making three additions of dry and two of buttermilk. Gently fold in strawberry mixture.
- Divide batter between two 8- x 4-inch (1.5 L) greased and floured loaf pans, smoothing tops. Bake in 350°F (180°C) oven for about 1 hour or until tester inserted in center comes out clean. Makes 2 loaves.

Cranberry Bread ▲

For pizzazz, garnish the top of this classic loaf with extra whole cranberries.

2 cups	all-purpose flour	500 mL
2/3 cup	granulated sugar	150 mL
1-1/2 tsp	baking powder	7 mL
3/4 tsp	salt	4 mL
1/2 tsp	baking soda	2 mL
1/4 cup	butter, softened	50 mL
3/4 cup	orange juice	175 mL
1 tsp	grated lemon rind	5 mL
1	egg	1
1 cup	cranberries (fresh or frozen), chopped	250 mL
	GARNISH	
6	whole cranberries	6

● In large bowl, combine flour, sugar, baking powder, salt and baking soda. With pastry blender or two knives, cut in butter until in coarse crumbs.

● Beat together orange juice, lemon rind and egg; pour over flour mixture. Sprinkle cranberries over top; stir just until dry ingredients are moistened. Pour into greased 9- x 5-inch (2 L) loaf pan.

● GARNISH: Carefully press whole cranberries halfway into batter in line lengthwise down center of loaf. Bake in 350°F (180°C) oven for 50 to 60 minutes or until tester inserted in center comes out clean. Makes 1 loaf.

Zucchini Loaf

3 cups	Best Muffin Mix (recipe, p. 20)	750 mL
1 cup	chopped pecans	250 mL
1/4 cup	packed brown sugar	50 mL
1 tbsp	cinnamon	15 mL
1/2 tsp	baking soda	2 mL
1/4 tsp	ground cloves	1 mL
1-1/2 cups	coarsely shredded zucchini	375 mL
1 cup	water	250 mL
1/3 cup	vegetable oil	75 mL
2	eggs	2
2 tsp	vanilla	10 mL
	Icing sugar	

● In large bowl, combine Best Muffin Mix, pecans, sugar, cinnamon, baking soda and cloves. Whisk together zucchini, water, oil, eggs and vanilla; pour over dry ingredients. Stir together just until moistened.

● Pour into greased 8- x 4-inch (1.5 L) loaf pan; bake in 350°F (180°C) oven for about 1 hour or until tester inserted in center comes out clean. Let cool completely. Dust with icing sugar. Makes 1 loaf.

Here's a sensible and delicious way to use up an abundance of zucchini — and get a healthy dose of vegetables at the same time!

Canuck Loaf

3 cups	Best Muffin Mix (recipe, p. 20)	750 mL
1 cup	chopped walnuts	250 mL
1/2 tsp	baking soda	2 mL
1 cup	applesauce	250 mL
1/2 cup	maple syrup	125 mL
1/3 cup	vegetable oil	75 mL
2	eggs	2
12	walnut halves	12

● In large bowl, combine Best Muffin Mix, chopped walnuts and baking soda. Whisk together applesauce, maple syrup, oil and eggs; pour over dry ingredients. Stir together just until moistened.

● Pour into greased 8- x 4-inch (1.5 L) loaf pan; arrange walnut halves on top. Bake in 350°F (180°C) oven for about 1 hour or until tester inserted in center comes out clean. Makes 1 loaf.

We call this Canuck because it contains two of Canada's finest ingredients — maple syrup and apples.

Orange Date Loaf

3 cups	Best Muffin Mix (recipe, p. 20)	750 mL
1/2 tsp	baking soda	2 mL
2 tsp	coarsely grated orange rind	10 mL
1 cup	orange juice	250 mL
1 cup	chopped dates	250 mL
1/3 cup	vegetable oil	75 mL
2	eggs	2
2 tsp	vanilla	10 mL
4	dates, quartered lengthwise	4

● In large bowl, combine Best Muffin Mix with baking soda. Whisk together orange rind and juice, chopped dates, oil, eggs and vanilla; pour over dry ingredients. Stir together just until moistened.

● Pour into greased 8- x 4-inch (1.5 L) loaf pan; arrange quartered dates in line lengthwise on top. Bake in 350°F (180°C) oven for about 1 hour or until tester inserted in center comes out clean. Makes 1 loaf.

Tangy orange and dense sweet dates mate happily in a loaf that's perfect for lunches and snacks.

Tender Biscuits and Scones

Whatever you call these tender golden morsels — scones, biscuits, tea biscuits or bannock — they are never-fail and a smashing addition to meals. They make superlative breakfast and snack fare, too.

Glazed Cinnamon Biscuit Buns ▶

Who can resist the fresh-baked flavor and aroma of an old-fashioned cinnamon and brown sugar roly-poly? These are so delicious and so easy to make, they're sure to become a weekend breakfast classic.

	Classic Tea Biscuits dough (recipe, p. 36)	
1/3 cup	packed brown sugar	75 mL
1/4 cup	butter, softened	50 mL
1 tsp	cinnamon	5 mL
1/3 cup	chopped pecans	75 mL
	GLAZE	
2 tbsp	corn syrup or liquid honey	25 mL
1/4 tsp	cinnamon	1 mL

- On lightly floured surface, roll out Classic Tea Biscuits dough to 16- x 10-inch (40 x 25 cm) rectangle. Combine brown sugar, butter and cinnamon; spread over dough. Sprinkle with pecans. Roll up into cylinder; cut into 12 slices.
- Place, cut side down, in greased 9-inch (1.5 L) round cake pan. Bake in 425°F (220°C) oven for 25 minutes or until lightly browned.
- GLAZE: Warm corn syrup with cinnamon over low heat; brush over baked buns. Makes 12 buns.

Biscuit Focaccia

Focaccia is an Italian flatbread sprinkled with herbs and olive oil. Making the bread with biscuit dough gets all the vibrant Mediterranean flavors to the table pronto.

	Classic Tea Biscuits dough (recipe, p. 36)	
1-1/2 tsp	dried rosemary	7 mL
4 tsp	extra virgin olive oil	20 mL
1 tbsp	freshly grated Parmesan cheese	15 mL
	Salt and pepper	

- Prepare Classic Tea Biscuits dough, adding 1 tsp (5 mL) dried rosemary to dry ingredients. On lightly floured surface, roll out to 1/4-inch (5 mm) thickness; transfer to lightly greased baking sheet.
- With knuckle, make indentations 1 inch (2.5 cm) apart in dough; brush with 1 tbsp (15 mL) of the oil. Sprinkle with Parmesan, remaining rosemary, and salt and pepper to taste. Bake in 400°F (200°C) oven for 20 to 25 minutes or until golden brown.
- Remove from oven; drizzle with remaining olive oil. Serve warm. Makes 1 flatbread.

Classic Tea Biscuits

Start with a tender, flaky tea biscuit — a simple and superlative pleasure. Add the extra flavor of cheese or dried fruit, if desired — or roll out the dough for deliciously different Glazed Cinnamon Biscuit Buns, herb-dappled Biscuit Focaccia (recipes, p. 34) or Chocolate Turnovers (recipe, next page).

2 cups	all-purpose flour	500 mL
1 tbsp	granulated sugar	15 mL
2 tsp	baking powder	10 mL
1/2 tsp	salt	2 ml
1/3 cup	shortening	75 mL
3/4 cup	milk	175 mL
	GLAZE	
2 tbsp	milk	25 mL

● In large bowl, combine flour, sugar, baking powder and salt. Using pastry blender or two knives, cut in shortening until crumbly. Add milk all at once; stir with fork to make soft, sticky dough.

● Turn out onto lightly floured surface; knead 8 to 10 times or until smooth. Gently pat out dough into 3/4-inch (2 cm) thick disc. Using 1-1/2-inch (4 cm) round cookie cutter, cut out biscuits; place on ungreased baking sheet.

● GLAZE: Brush tops with milk; bake in 400°F (200°C) oven for 17 to 20 minutes or until puffed and bottoms are golden. Makes 1 dozen biscuits.

VARIATIONS

● CHEESE BISCUITS: After cutting in shortening, stir in 1 cup (250 mL) shredded extra-old Cheddar cheese and 1/2 tsp (2 mL) pepper.

● DRIED FRUIT BISCUITS: After cutting in shortening, add 1/2 cup (125 mL) raisins, dried cranberries, dried cherries or dried blueberries. Sprinkle biscuits with cinnamon to taste before baking.

FOR PERFECT BISCUITS EVERY TIME

1 Because biscuits are rich in fat, you don't need to grease the baking sheet. You can leave the sheet ungreased or sprinkle baking sheet lightly with all-purpose flour.

2 Always pour liquid ingredients over the entire surface of the dry ingredients, tossing lightly with fork to incorporate dry into wet without overworking the flour.

3 When wet and dry are combined, knead the dough lightly about 10 turns, either in the bowl or on floured counter, to complete the blending of wet and dry.

4 Handle the dough as little as possible. For best results, reroll scraps only once, pressing any bits left over into a "cook's biscuit" or sprinkling with sugar and cinnamon for quickie cinnamon treats.

5 To prevent dough from sticking to the cookie cutter, dip cutter into flour before cutting each biscuit.

6 To save time cutting biscuits and rerolling scraps, roll or pat dough into rectangle or square shape and use knife to cut biscuits into squares or diamonds.

7 To ensure even browning and baking, make each biscuit the same size and shape.

8 For soft-sided biscuits, snuggle them together in a cake pan. For crisp, golden biscuits, bake on baking sheets, each biscuit well separated from the others.

9 For glossy golden biscuits, brush tops with milk, cream or beaten egg. Or, try an egg yolk beaten with 1 tbsp (15 mL) water to brush over each biscuit. Then, add a sprinkle of sugar, herbs, or sesame or poppy seeds.

10 To remove the sticky batter from bowls and fork, first rinse with cold water before washing in hot soapy water.

Chocolate Turnovers

	Classic Tea Biscuits dough (recipe, p. 36)	
4 oz	semisweet chocolate, coarsely chopped	125 g
1	egg yolk	1
2 tbsp	granulated sugar	25 mL

● On lightly floured surface, roll out Classic Tea Biscuits dough to 16- x 8-inch (40 x 20 cm) rectangle. Cut into eight 4-inch (10 cm) squares. Divide chocolate among centers of squares; fold dough over to form triangle.

● Place triangles on ungreased baking sheet. Brush with egg yolk; sprinkle with sugar. Bake in 400°F (200°C) oven for 20 minutes or until bottoms are golden. Makes 8 turnovers.

These sweet treats are a quick and easy version of the French classic, pain au chocolat. *They're equally delicious with morning coffee or an afternoon cup of tea.*

Herb Scones with a Light Touch

1-3/4 cups	all-purpose flour	425 mL
4 tsp	baking powder	20 mL
1 tbsp	granulated sugar	15 mL
1 tbsp	chopped fresh chives or green onion	15 mL
1 tbsp	chopped fresh parsley	15 mL
3/4 tsp	salt	4 mL
1/2 tsp	dried thyme	2 mL
1/4 cup	butter, cubed	50 mL
1 cup	plain yogurt	250 mL

● In large bowl, combine flour, baking powder, sugar, chives, parsley, salt and thyme. Using pastry blender or two knives, cut in butter until crumbly. Using fork, stir in yogurt. Knead about 5 times or until smooth.

● On lightly floured surface, roll out to 1-inch (2.5 cm) thickness. Using 2-inch (5 cm) round cutter, cut out circles; place on ungreased baking sheet.

● Bake in 425°F (220°C) oven for 10 to 12 minutes or until lightly browned. Makes 12 scones.

Yogurt replaces most of the fat in these irresistible scones. Serve with soup, stews or brunch egg dishes.

Heart-Shaped Butter Scones

2 cups	all-purpose flour	500 mL
1/3 cup	granulated sugar	75 mL
1 tbsp	baking powder	15 mL
1/2 tsp	baking soda	2 mL
Pinch	salt	Pinch
1/2 cup	butter, cubed	125 mL
1-1/2 cups	plain yogurt	375 mL
	TOPPING	
2 tsp	granulated sugar	10 mL

● In large bowl, combine flour, sugar, baking powder, baking soda and salt. With fingertips, rub in butter until in tiny bits. Using fork, stir in yogurt to make soft dough.

● On lightly floured surface, gather dough into ball; pat out into 1/2-inch (1 cm) thick disc. Using floured 3- or 4-inch (8 or 10 cm) heart-shaped cookie cutter, cut out shapes, rerolling scraps once. Place 1 inch (2.5 cm) apart on ungreased baking sheets.

● TOPPING: Sprinkle sugar over dough. Bake in 425°F (220°C) oven for 12 to 15 minutes or until puffed and lightly browned. Makes 12 scones.

Scones beg to be served warm, buttered and spread with jam, marmalade or honey to drip off the warm crusty edges. You can vary the shape to honor the occasion — shamrocks for St. Patrick's, bells for Christmas, maple leaves for Canada Day.

Canadian Living's Best Scone Mix

"Better, simply so much better than bought mixes" is how our Test Kitchen describes this mix for an unbelievably light scone with a tender, golden crust. The secret is cake-and-pastry flour. The mix also includes skim milk powder, a very handy ingredient that ensures you can make scones or biscuits even if you've run out of milk.

9 cups	cake-and-pastry flour	2.25 L
1 cup	skim milk powder	250 mL
1/2 cup	granulated sugar	125 mL
1/4 cup	baking powder	50 mL
1 tbsp	salt	15 mL
2 tsp	baking soda	10 mL
1 lb	shortening	500 g

- In large bowl, combine flour, milk powder, sugar, baking powder, salt and baking soda. Using pastry blender, cut in shortening until mixture is in fine crumbs. Transfer to airtight container; store in refrigerator for up to 2 months. Stir well before using. Makes about 15 cups (3.75 L).

TIP: When measuring large quantities of dry ingredients, measure each into separate bowl; that way, if you lose count, you can recheck before mixing ingredients.

Golden Scones ◀

Fluffy, hot from the oven and ready for a dab of jam, a shower of berries or a slice of cheese, these scones are ideal for everything from shortcake dessert to serving with soups and salads. Why not try all three tasty variations?

3 cups	Best Scone Mix	750 mL
2/3 cup	water	150 mL

- In bowl and using fork, quickly stir Best Scone Mix with water until sticky dough forms. Turn out onto lightly floured surface; knead 6 times.
- Press into 1-inch (2.5 cm) thick round. Using lightly floured 2-inch (5 cm) round cutter, cut out circles, rerolling scraps once.
- Bake on baking sheet in 450°F (230°C) oven for 10 to 12 minutes or until golden brown. *(Scones can be individually wrapped and frozen in airtight container for up to 2 weeks.)* Makes 13 scones.

VARIATIONS

- CHEESE SCONES: Add 1/2 cup (125 mL) freshly grated Parmesan or Cheddar cheese to dry ingredients.
- HERB SCONES: Add 2 tbsp (25 mL) chopped fresh herbs (or 2 tsp/10 mL dried) to dry ingredients.
- SWEET RAISIN SCONES: Add 2 tsp (10 mL) cinnamon and 3/4 cup (175 mL) raisins to dry ingredients.

Popovers

Serve these quick-to-make popovers piping hot with butter and jam for breakfast, alongside soup or salad for a lunchtime treat — or fill with your favorite hearty stew for a satisfying supper.

1 cup	all-purpose flour	250 mL
1/2 tsp	salt	2 mL
1 cup	milk	250 mL
3	eggs	3
2 tbsp	vegetable oil	25 mL

● In bowl, combine flour with salt. Whisk together milk, eggs and oil; gradually whisk into flour mixture until smooth.

● Spoon into 8 greased custard cups, filling half full, or 10 muffin cups. Bake in 450°F (230°C) oven for 10 minutes. Reduce heat to 375°F (190°C); bake for about 30 minutes longer or until crusty and deep golden brown. Serve immediately. Makes 8 large or 10 medium popovers.

VARIATION

● HERBED PARMESAN POPOVERS: Add 3 tbsp (50 mL) freshly grated Parmesan cheese and 1 tsp (5 mL) dried thyme to dry ingredients.

Cheese Crispies

Vancouver's Margaret Murphy makes up many batches of these nippy appetizers for the annual Christmas bazaar at Hycroft, the historic home of the University Women's Club of Vancouver.

1 cup	butter, softened	250 mL
1	container (250 g) cold-pack Cheddar cheese	1
1/2 tsp	Worcestershire sauce	2 mL
Dash	hot pepper sauce	Dash
4 cups	crispy rice cereal	1 L
1-1/2 cups	all-purpose flour	375 mL
1/2 tsp	dry mustard	2 mL
1/4 tsp	each salt and paprika	1 mL

● In large bowl, beat together butter, Cheddar, Worcestershire and hot pepper sauces until fluffy. Combine cereal, flour, mustard, salt and paprika; blend into butter mixture with hands.

● Roll into 1-1/4-inch (3 cm) balls; place about 3 inches (8 cm) apart on greased baking sheet. With fork, flatten to 1/2-inch (1 cm) thickness.

● Bake in 400°F (200°C) oven for about 8 minutes or until golden brown underneath and crisp. *(Crispies can be stored in airtight container for 1 day or frozen for up to 1 week.)* Makes 4 dozen crispies.

Normaway Oatcakes

Oatcakes — shingle-shaped oatmeal crackers that beg for butter and honey — are sure to be found in any Nova Scotia breadbasket. The Normaway Inn, nestled in Cape Breton's Margaree River valley, serves this stellar version.

3 cups	rolled oats	750 mL
1-1/2 cups	all-purpose flour	375 mL
1/2 cup	packed brown sugar	125 mL
1/2 tsp	salt	2 mL
1/2 tsp	baking soda	2 mL
1 cup	shortening	250 mL
1/2 cup	cold water	125 mL

● In large bowl, combine rolled oats, flour, sugar, salt and baking soda. With pastry blender or two knives, cut in shortening until crumbly. Gradually sprinkle with water, tossing with fork to make sticky dough. Gather into ball; divide in half.

● On floured pastry cloth and using stockinette-covered rolling pin, roll out each half to 12- x 9-inch (30 x 23 cm) rectangle. Cut into 3-inch (8 cm) squares; cut each diagonally in half, if desired.

● Bake on greased baking sheets in 350°F (180°C) oven for 10 to 15 minutes or until golden brown on bottom. Makes 24 oatcakes.

Whole Wheat Soda Bread

2 cups	whole wheat flour	500 mL
1 cup	(approx) all-purpose flour	250 mL
1/2 cup	currants	125 mL
2 tbsp	granulated sugar	25 mL
1 tsp	baking powder	5 mL
1 tsp	baking soda	5 mL
1/2 tsp	salt	2 mL
2 tbsp	butter	25 mL
1-1/2 cups	buttermilk	375 mL

● In large bowl, combine whole wheat and all-purpose flours, currants, sugar, baking powder, baking soda and salt. With pastry blender or two knives, cut in butter until crumbly. Using fork, stir in buttermilk just until moistened.

● On lightly floured surface, gather dough into ball; knead lightly 10 times. Place on greased baking sheet; gently pat out dough into 1-1/2-inch (4 cm) thick disc. Dust generously with all-purpose flour.

● With sharp knife, score top of loaf with large X. Bake in 375°F (190°C) oven for 45 minutes or until golden and tester inserted in center comes out clean. Makes 1 loaf.

The cross on top is a distinctive part of soda bread, which originated in Ireland. It dates back to ancient times, but serves a purpose in the baking process by allowing the bread to expand.

Blueberry Honey Soda Bread ▼

3 cups	all-purpose flour	750 mL
1 cup	whole wheat flour	250 mL
1 tbsp	baking powder	15 mL
1-1/2 tsp	salt	7 mL
1 tsp	baking soda	5 mL
1/4 cup	butter	50 mL
1 cup	blueberries	250 mL
2	eggs	2
1-1/2 cups	buttermilk	375 mL
1/4 cup	liquid honey	50 mL

● In large bowl, combine all-purpose and whole wheat flours, baking powder, salt and baking soda. With pastry blender or two knives, cut in butter until crumbly. Gently stir in blueberries.

● In small bowl, beat eggs; whisk in buttermilk and honey. Using fork, stir into flour mixture to make soft dough.

● On lightly floured surface, gather dough into ball; knead lightly 10 times. Place on greased baking sheet; flatten into 9-inch (23 cm) round. With sharp knife, score top of loaf with large X. Bake in 350°F (180°C) oven for 1 hour or until golden and tester inserted in center comes out clean. Makes 1 loaf.

Warm from the oven, soda breads are hard to match for their fine texture and good, real-bread taste. An excellent replacement for yeast breads, they do honor to a plate of your favorite cheeses. Blueberries add color and a taste of summer.

No-Fuss Cakes

Chocolate, honey, carrot, cherry, coffee and ginger — all the crowd-pleasing flavors are here, ready to whip up into easy cake treats for family, friends and neighbors.

Chocolate Carrot Cupcakes ▶

This delicious new twist on carrot cake makes a dozen cupcakes or a large pan cake that's ideal for the gang. For special occasions, add a tasty cream cheese icing and sprinkles.

2 cups	all-purpose flour	500 mL
2/3 cup	sifted unsweetened cocoa powder	150 mL
2 tsp	baking powder	10 mL
1 tsp	baking soda	5 mL
1 tsp	each cinnamon and nutmeg	5 mL
1/2 tsp	salt	2 mL
1/2 tsp	ground cloves	2 mL
4	eggs	4
1 cup	packed brown sugar	250 mL
1 cup	vegetable oil	250 mL
3/4 cup	unsweetened applesauce	175 mL
1/2 cup	granulated sugar	125 mL
3 cups	grated carrots (about 6 large)	750 mL
2/3 cup	chopped nuts or raisins	150 mL
	Vanilla Cream Cheese Icing (recipe, p. 45)	

● In large bowl, stir together flour, cocoa, baking powder, baking soda, cinnamon, nutmeg, salt and cloves. Whisk together eggs, brown sugar, oil, applesauce and granulated sugar; stir into dry ingredients and beat for 1 minute. Stir in carrots and nuts.

● Spoon into greased or paper-lined muffin cups. Bake in 350°F (180°C) oven for 20 to 25 minutes or until cake tester inserted in center comes out clean. Let cool completely. Spread Vanilla Cream Cheese Icing over tops. Makes 2 dozen cupcakes.

TIP: To bake as cake, pour batter into greased and floured 13- x 9-inch (3.5 L) cake pan. Bake for about 1 hour or until cake tester inserted in center comes out clean. Let cool in pan on rack for 10 minutes; turn out onto rack to cool completely.

MIXING UP A CAKE

The electric mixer, for the last 40 years a fixture in Canadian kitchens, has transformed cake making from a special-occasion treat to an effortless everyday delight.

● For the cakes in this book, a hand-held electric mixer is sufficient. For best results, use a real mixing bowl with straight sides that keep the batter within the action of the beaters.

Carrot Cupcakes

Most carrot cakes have more oil and sugar than they really need. These tasty cupcakes are an exception. Pack them into school lunches for a treat that isn't just empty calories.

3	eggs	3
3/4 cup	packed brown sugar	175 mL
1/2 cup	vegetable oil	125 mL
1/2 cup	orange juice	125 mL
2 tsp	vanilla	10 mL
2 cups	grated carrots	500 mL
1 cup	all-purpose flour	250 mL
1 cup	whole wheat flour	250 mL
1/2 cup	crushed pineapple	125 mL
2 tsp	baking soda	10 mL
2 tsp	cinnamon	10 mL
2 tsp	grated orange rind	10 mL
1/2 tsp	nutmeg	2 mL
	ORANGE CREAM CHEESE ICING	
8 oz	light cream cheese, softened	250 g
1/4 cup	icing sugar	50 mL
1 tsp	grated orange rind	5 mL
4 tsp	orange juice	20 mL

- In food processor, blend together eggs, sugar, oil, orange juice and vanilla. Add carrots, all-purpose and whole wheat flours, pineapple, baking soda, cinnamon, orange rind and nutmeg; blend for 20 seconds, scraping down sides halfway through.
- Spoon about 1/3 cup (75 mL) batter into each well-greased muffin cup. Bake in 350°F (180°C) oven for 35 to 40 minutes or until cake tester inserted in center comes out clean. Let cool in pan.
- ORANGE CREAM CHEESE ICING: In small bowl, beat cream cheese with sugar until fluffy; stir in orange rind and juice. Spread over cupcakes. Makes 12 cupcakes.

Fudgy Cheesecake Cupcakes

This is cake-making at its simplest. No beating until creamy, very little measuring, and the batter's all in one bowl. A perfect recipe for junior bakers!

1-1/2 cups	all-purpose flour	375 mL
1 cup	granulated sugar	250 mL
1/4 cup	unsweetened cocoa powder, sifted	50 mL
1 tsp	baking soda	5 mL
Pinch	salt	Pinch
1 cup	water	250 mL
1/3 cup	vegetable oil	75 mL
1 tbsp	cider vinegar	15 mL
1-1/2 tsp	vanilla	7 mL
	TOPPING	
4 oz	cream cheese, softened	125 g
3 tbsp	granulated sugar	45 mL
1	egg yolk	1
Pinch	salt	Pinch
1/2 cup	miniature chocolate chips	125 mL

- TOPPING: In bowl, beat cream cheese with sugar until fluffy. Beat in egg yolk and salt until smooth. Fold in chocolate chips. Set aside.
- In large bowl, stir together flour, sugar, cocoa, baking soda and salt; make well in center. Pour in water, oil, vinegar and vanilla; whisk until combined.
- Spoon into greased or paper-lined muffins cups, filling halfway to top. Spoon 1 tbsp (15 mL) topping over each. Bake in 350°F (180°C) oven for 20 to 25 minutes or until tops spring back when lightly pressed. *(Cupcakes can be stored in airtight containers in refrigerator for up to 3 days.)* Makes 15 cupcakes.

Vanilla Butter Icing

1/2 cup	butter, softened	125 mL
2 tbsp	milk	25 mL
2 tsp	vanilla	10 mL
2 cups	sifted icing sugar	500 mL

● In bowl, beat together butter, milk and vanilla at medium-low speed for 30 seconds or until creamy. Add 1 cup (250 mL) of the icing sugar; beat for 30 seconds. Add remaining sugar; beat for about 2 minutes or until light and fluffy. Makes 1-3/4 cups (425 mL).

VARIATIONS

● PISTACHIO BUTTER ICING: Toast 1/2 cup (125 mL) chopped unsalted shelled pistachios in 350°F (180°C) oven for 10 minutes; let cool. Fold into finished icing.

● COFFEE BUTTER ICING: Omit vanilla. Dissolve 2 tbsp (25 mL) instant coffee granules in the milk.

● MAPLE WALNUT BUTTER ICING: Substitute 2 tsp (10 mL) maple extract for vanilla. Toast 1/2 cup (125 mL) chopped walnuts in 350°F (180°C) oven for 10 minutes; let cool. Fold into finished icing.

These icings make enough to cover the top of one 9-inch (23 cm) cake, and any combination with cakes or cupcakes is pleasing. For celebrations, add chopped nuts, sprinkles, shaved chocolate, crushed chocolate toffee bars or other treats to a plain icing.

Chocolate Cream Cheese Icing

6 oz	semisweet chocolate, coarsely chopped	175 g
1	pkg (250 g) cream cheese, softened	1
1/4 cup	milk	50 mL
1/4 cup	sifted icing sugar	50 mL

● In bowl, melt chocolate over hot (not boiling) water; let cool to room temperature. In separate bowl, beat cream cheese with milk at medium speed for 30 seconds or until blended. Add icing sugar; beat for 30 seconds. Add chocolate; beat at low speed for 1-1/2 minutes or until smooth and creamy. Makes 2 cups (500 mL).

Both the cream cheese and chocolate should be at room temperature before combining or else the chocolate will harden and not blend in properly.

Vanilla Cream Cheese Icing

1	pkg (250 g) cream cheese, softened	1
2 tsp	vanilla	10 mL
1 cup	sifted icing sugar	250 mL

● In bowl, beat cream cheese with vanilla at medium speed for 30 seconds or until blended. Add icing sugar; beat for 1-1/2 minutes or until smooth and creamy. Makes 1-1/2 cups (375 mL).

VARIATION

● CITRUS CREAM CHEESE ICING: Omit vanilla. Add 1 tsp (5 mL) each grated orange and lemon rind and 1-1/2 tsp (7 mL) lemon juice to the cream cheese.

The creaminess of this icing makes it a perfect topping for the Ginger Spice Cake (p. 47), especially with a sprinkle of extra chopped crystallized ginger.

Canadian Living's Best Cake Mix

One easy snacking cake mix, developed in the Canadian Living Test Kitchen, lets you get creative with chocolate, spices, poppy seeds and vanilla. Quick to assemble, this mix is a bonus for busy schedules. *(See p. 45 for a selection of flavorful icings.)*

8 cups	cake-and-pastry flour	2 L
6 cups	granulated sugar	1.5 L
1/4 cup	baking powder	50 mL
2 tsp	salt	10 mL

- In large bowl, mix together flour, sugar, baking powder and salt until well combined. Transfer to airtight container; store in cool, dry place for up to 2 months. Stir well before using. Makes about 14 cups (3.5 L).

Chocolate Mocha Cake

Buttermilk makes the texture of this cake light, while a hint of coffee enriches its fudgy chocolate flavor.

2 tbsp	hot water	25 mL
1 tbsp	instant coffee granules	15 mL
3-1/3 cups	Best Cake Mix	825 mL
3/4 cup	buttermilk	175 mL
1/2 cup	sifted unsweetened cocoa powder	125 mL
1/2 tsp	baking soda	2 mL
1/2 cup	vegetable oil	125 mL
2	eggs	2
2 tsp	vanilla	10 mL

- In small bowl, stir water with coffee; let cool.
- In large bowl and using electric mixer at medium speed, beat Best Cake Mix, buttermilk, coffee, cocoa and baking soda for 2 minutes. Add oil, eggs and vanilla; reduce speed to low and beat for 1 minute.
- Pour into greased 9-inch (2.5 L) square cake pan; bake in 375°F (190°C) oven for 35 minutes or until cake tester inserted in center comes out clean. Let cool in pan on rack. Makes 12 servings.

White Vanilla Cake

Great for shortcake, ready for a trifle or your choice of icing, this simple vanilla-scented cake will satisfy all the "just plain, please" fans.

3-1/3 cups	Best Cake Mix	825 mL
3/4 cup	milk	175 mL
1/2 cup	vegetable oil	125 mL
2	eggs	2
2 tsp	vanilla	10 mL

- In large bowl and using electric mixer at medium speed, beat Best Cake Mix with milk for 2 minutes. Add oil, eggs and vanilla; reduce speed to low and beat for 1 minute.
- Pour into greased 9-inch (2.5 L) square cake pan; bake in 375°F (190°C) oven for 30 minutes or until cake tester inserted in center comes out clean. Let cool in pan on rack. Makes 12 servings.

Ginger Spice Cake

3-1/3 cups	Best Cake Mix	825 mL
3/4 cup	plain yogurt	175 mL
2 tbsp	chopped crystallized ginger	25 mL
1-1/2 tsp	cinnamon	7 mL
1 tsp	ground ginger	5 mL
Pinch	ground cloves	Pinch
1/2 cup	vegetable oil	125 mL
2	eggs	2
2 tsp	vanilla	10 mL

● In large bowl and using electric mixer at medium speed, beat Best Cake Mix, yogurt, chopped ginger, cinnamon, ground ginger and cloves for 2 minutes. Add oil, eggs and vanilla; reduce speed to low and beat for 1 minute.

● Pour into greased 9-inch (2.5 L) cake pan; bake in 375°F (190°C) oven for 35 minutes or until cake tester inserted in center comes out clean. Let cool in pan on rack. Makes 12 servings.

When the fragrant aroma of this ginger-studded spice cake fills the house, don't be surprised if everyone hurries to the kitchen for the first still-warm piece!

Citrus Poppy Seed Cake

3-1/3 cups	Best Cake Mix	825 mL
3/4 cup	milk	175 mL
2 tbsp	poppy seeds	25 mL
1 tbsp	grated orange rind	15 mL
2 tsp	grated lemon rind	10 mL
1/2 cup	vegetable oil	125 mL
2	eggs	2
2 tsp	vanilla	10 mL

● In large bowl and using electric mixer at medium speed, beat Best Cake Mix, milk, poppy seeds and orange and lemon rind for 2 minutes. Add oil, eggs and vanilla; reduce speed to low and beat for 1 minute.

● Pour into greased 9-inch (2.5 L) cake pan; bake in 375°F (190°C) oven for 35 minutes or until cake tester inserted in center comes out clean. Let cool in pan on rack. Makes 12 servings.

This easy cake blends the freshness of lemon and orange with the nutty crunch of poppy seeds. The batter is particularly good in cupcakes (see box, below).

BEST CAKE BASICS

Measuring

● To measure dry ingredients properly, spoon into dry measure until heaping, without packing or tapping; level off with straight edge of knife.

Beating

● Beating times for cakes should be followed precisely. If time is shortened, cake will lack structure; if lengthened, cake will be tough.

Making Cupcakes

● Bake White Vanilla, Chocolate Mocha and Citrus Poppy Seed Cakes as cupcakes by dividing batter among 18 paper-lined muffin cups; bake in 375°F (190°C) oven for 20 minutes or until cake tester inserted in center comes out clean.

Quick Icing

● Make a quick icing for White Vanilla and Chocolate Mocha Cakes by topping cake with 3/4 cup (175 mL) chocolate chips as soon as it is removed from oven; let chocolate melt, then spread smoothly.

Storing

● Cakes can be well wrapped and frozen for up to 2 weeks.

Spiced Honey Cake ▸

Fragrant with cinnamon, cloves and nutmeg, dark and rich with coffee, this walnut-studded honey cake is traditionally served at Rosh Hashanah, the Jewish New Year, and celebrates the hope for a sweet and satisfying year.

1-1/3 cups	liquid honey	325 mL
1 cup	strong coffee	250 mL
1 tbsp	grated orange rind	15 mL
2-3/4 cups	all-purpose flour	675 mL
2 tsp	baking powder	10 mL
1 tsp	baking soda	5 mL
1 tsp	cinnamon	5 mL
1/2 tsp	nutmeg	2 mL
1/4 tsp	each ground cloves and ginger	1 mL
Pinch	salt	Pinch
1 cup	chopped walnuts	250 mL
4	eggs	4
1/4 cup	vegetable oil	50 mL
1 cup	granulated sugar	250 mL
	Icing sugar	

- In small saucepan, bring honey just to boil; remove from heat. Stir in coffee and orange rind; let cool slightly.
- Meanwhile, in bowl, stir together flour, baking powder, baking soda, cinnamon, nutmeg, cloves, ginger and salt. Remove 2 tbsp (25 mL) and toss with walnuts; set aside.
- In large bowl, beat eggs until lemon-colored; beat in oil. Gradually beat in sugar until pale and thickened, about 3 minutes.
- Using whisk, alternately fold dry and honey mixtures into egg mixture, making three additions of dry and two of honey mixture. Fold in reserved walnuts.
- Pour into greased nonstick 10-inch (3 L) Bundt pan. Bake in 325°F (160°C) oven for about 1 hour or until cake springs back when lightly pressed and cake tester inserted in center comes out clean. Let cool in pan on rack for 30 minutes; invert onto rack to cool completely. Sift icing sugar over top. Makes 12 servings.

VARIATIONS

- FRUITED HONEY CAKE: Substitute raisins or candied citron or almonds for the walnuts.
- SPIRITED HONEY CAKE: Substitute 3 tbsp (50 mL) cognac for 3 tbsp (50 mL) of the coffee.

TIPS:

- Whisking the honey mixture into the eggs prevents it from sinking to the bottom. However, don't overwhisk or you'll end up with an unevenly textured cake.
- If you use a Bundt pan without nonstick coating, loosen edges of cake with knife before inverting onto rack; then rap pan sharply with wooden spoon before removing pan.
- Cake can also be baked and cooled in two 9- x 5-inch (2 L) loaf pans (with waxed paper-lined bottoms).

HONEY IN CAKES

- For a more distinct honey flavor, choose a full-flavored honey such as amber buckwheat. For a milder honey flavor, pale golden honeys such as clover, fireweed or alfalfa are recommended.
- To measure honey, lightly oil the measuring cup before filling with honey. The honey will pour right out of the cup without sticking.

SPICE UP YOUR BAKING

Freshness

- Fresh spices are crucial to the taste of fine baking. It's a waste of good eggs, nuts, butter and flour if spices are tired and faded.

Buying Spices

- Buy in quantities that suit your baking style — larger if you bake every week, smaller if baking is an occasional pleasure.
- Generally, bottled spices are more expensive than bulk spices or spices in bags, but richer in flavor and aroma and worth every penny.

Storage

- Store spices away from heat and light. A drawer deep enough to hold jars upright is ideal — especially if you label the tops of the jars and organize the spices alphabetically.

Whole Spices

- Whole spices are always more flavorful — whole nutmegs, cardamom pods, blades of mace and even cinnamon sticks — especially if you have a spice grinder or can clean out a coffee grinder whenever you want a fresh batch of spices.

Mace

- Mace is the rusty orange-colored web-like covering of whole nutmegs. If you don't have mace, simply use more nutmeg.

Cardamom

- Cardamom is a spice much favored in Indian and Scandinavian cooking, often used in breads and cakes in Scandinavia, and even used to perfume tea in India.
- Cardamom's aroma and taste are compelling. If ground cardamom is unavailable and you can buy cardamom pods, buy the green or white pods rather than the larger, coarser brown ones.
- You only need your hands and possibly a small knife to break apart the papery pods and take out the dark seeds. These seeds are easy to grind in a mortar and pestle or coffee or spice grinder. Look for cardamom pods in Indian grocery stores.

Spiced Carrot Cake

Puréed carrots add a beautifully rich burnt-orange color to a cake that's aromatic with spices. For a change of taste, substitute canned puréed pumpkin for the carrots.

1/2 cup	butter, softened	125 mL
1 cup	granulated sugar	250 mL
2	eggs	2
1 tsp	vanilla extract	5 mL
1 tbsp	grated orange rind	15 mL
1 cup	puréed cooked carrots	250 mL
1/4 cup	plain yogurt	50 mL
2 cups	all-purpose flour	500 mL
2 tsp	cinnamon	10 mL
1 tsp	ground cardamom	5 mL
1 tsp	baking soda	5 mL
1/4 tsp	each nutmeg and mace	1 mL
	Sifted icing sugar (optional)	

- In bowl, beat butter with sugar until fluffy. Beat in eggs, one at a time. Beat in vanilla and orange rind.
- Combine carrots and yogurt. Stir together flour, cinnamon, cardamom, baking soda, nutmeg and mace. Add to butter mixture alternately with carrot mixture, making three additions of dry and two of carrot mixture.
- Pour into greased 10-inch (3 L) Bundt pan. Bake in 350°F (180°C) oven for 40 to 45 minutes or until cake tester inserted in center comes out clean. Let cool in pan on rack for 10 minutes; turn out onto rack to cool completely. Sprinkle with icing sugar (if using). Makes 12 to 16 servings.

TIP: To arrive at 1 cup (250 mL) puréed carrots, either steam, boil or microwave 2 cups (500 mL) sliced carrots (6 medium) until tender, then drain and purée in blender, food processor or food mill. Or, take it easy and use a 7-1/2 oz (213 mL) jar of strained baby food carrots.

Pumpkin Gingerbread Snacking Cake

1-1/2 cups	granulated sugar	375 mL
2	eggs	2
1 cup	pumpkin purée	250 mL
1/2 cup	vegetable oil	125 mL
1/2 cup	buttermilk	125 mL
1-3/4 cups	all-purpose flour	425 mL
1 tsp	baking soda	5 mL
1 tsp	ginger	5 mL
1/2 tsp	each salt, cinnamon, nutmeg, ground cloves and allspice	2 mL
1/4 tsp	baking powder	1 mL
	Icing sugar	

● In bowl, beat together granulated sugar, eggs, pumpkin, oil and buttermilk until smooth. Stir together flour, baking soda, ginger, salt, cinnamon, nutmeg, cloves, allspice and baking powder; stir into pumpkin mixture until blended.

● Pour into greased 9-inch (2.5 L) square cake pan. Bake in 350°F (180°C) oven for about 35 minutes or until top springs back when lightly touched. Let cool in pan on rack. Dust with icing sugar. Makes 16 servings.

All the flavors of pumpkin pie come together in this easy and delicious cake — great with mugs of steaming mulled cider after raking the leaves or with café au lait to welcome a lazy weekend morning.

Applesauce Snacking Cake

3/4 cup	all-purpose flour	175 mL
2/3 cup	whole wheat flour	150 mL
3/4 tsp	baking soda	4 mL
1 tsp	cinnamon	5 mL
1/2 tsp	ginger	2 mL
Pinch	each ground cloves and salt	Pinch
1 cup	applesauce	250 mL
1/4 cup	packed brown sugar	50 mL
1/4 cup	fancy molasses	50 mL
1/4 cup	vegetable oil	50 mL
2	eggs	2
1 cup	raisins	250 mL
	ICING	
2/3 cup	icing sugar	150 mL
1 tbsp	apple juice	15 mL

● In bowl, stir together all-purpose and whole wheat flours, baking soda, cinnamon, ginger, cloves and salt. Whisk together applesauce, sugar, molasses, oil and eggs; pour over flour mixture along with raisins. Stir together just until combined.

● Pour into greased 9-inch (2.5 L) square cake pan, smoothing top. Bake in 350°F (180°C) oven for 20 to 25 minutes or until cake tester inserted in center comes out clean. Let cool in pan on rack.

● ICING: Whisk together icing sugar and juice; drizzle over cooled cake. Makes 16 servings.

Applesauce keeps this all-season cake moist and ready to enjoy with hot chocolate or cider in winter, or with iced tea when the mercury climbs.

HOMEMADE APPLESAUCE

A bowl of applesauce in the fridge is a wonderful convenience for quick desserts, snacks and breakfasts. Applesauce is also a handy ingredient in baking. While perfectly good applesauce is available in the supermarket, it's also easy to make at home — and the just-made apple-fresh taste is certainly worth it.

● Peel, core and slice 8 apples (3 lb/1.5 kg) thickly. Place apples and 1/2 cup (125 mL) water in heavy saucepan; cover and cook over medium heat, stirring occasionally, for 20 minutes or until very tender. (Alternatively, in microwaveable casserole or large measure, microwave at High, stirring twice, for 12 minutes or until very tender. Let stand for 5 minutes.)

● Purée apples in food processor or blender, or press through food mill. Makes 4 cups (1 L) applesauce.

● If desired, sweeten to taste with sugar while applesauce is still warm. Add a sprinkle of cinnamon, too.

Apple Almond Cake ▶

Fancy enough to serve as a dinner-party dessert, this pretty almond-topped cake brings just as much pleasure at brunches and morning coffee occasions.

1-1/2 cups	all-purpose flour	375 mL
3/4 cup	granulated sugar	175 mL
1-1/2 tsp	baking powder	7 mL
1/2 tsp	baking soda	2 mL
1/4 tsp	salt	1 mL
2	eggs	2
2/3 cup	plain yogurt	150 mL
1/4 cup	butter, melted	50 mL
1/2 tsp	almond extract	2 mL
3	apples, peeled and thinly sliced	3
	TOPPING	
3 tbsp	sliced blanched almonds	45 mL
2 tbsp	granulated sugar	25 mL
1/2 tsp	cinnamon	2 mL

● In bowl, stir together flour, sugar, baking powder, baking soda and salt. In separate bowl, beat eggs; stir in yogurt, butter and almond extract. Stir into flour mixture just until combined. Pour into greased 9-inch (2.5 L) springform pan. Arrange apples over batter.

● TOPPING: Combine almonds, sugar and cinnamon; sprinkle over apples. Bake in 350°F (180°C) oven for 1 hour or until cake tester inserted in center comes out clean. Makes 8 servings.

Microwave Pineapple Upside-Down Cake

The marvel of it all — pineapple slices start out under the batter, but end up as a golden glazed top over a fine-textured and not-too-sweet cake. If you have never tried an upside-down cake, this is an excellent one to make as your debut. And in the microwave, too!

1-1/3 cups	all-purpose flour	325 mL
1/2 cup	granulated sugar	125 mL
1-1/2 tsp	baking powder	7 mL
1/4 tsp	salt	1 mL
2/3 cup	milk	150 mL
1/3 cup	butter, melted	75 mL
1	egg	1
1 tsp	vanilla	5 mL
	TOPPING	
3 tbsp	butter	45 mL
1/2 cup	packed brown sugar	125 mL
4	slices fresh pineapple (or unsweetened canned)	4
1/4 cup	chopped pecans	50 mL

● TOPPING: In 8-inch (2 L) square microwaveable baking dish, microwave butter at High for 1 minute or until melted. Stir in sugar; microwave at High for 2 to 3 minutes or until bubbly. Place 1 pineapple ring at center; cut remaining rings in half and arrange around center slice.

● Microwave at High for 2 minutes. Spoon pecans evenly among pineapple; set aside.

● In bowl, stir together flour, sugar, baking powder and salt; make well in center. Beat together milk, butter, egg and vanilla; pour into well and stir just until combined. Spoon over pineapple mixture, spreading evenly.

● Place on microwaveable rack or inverted saucer; microwave at Medium (50%), rotating twice, for 5 minutes. Microwave at High, rotating once, for 2 to 3 minutes or until cake tester inserted in center comes out clean.

● Let stand directly on flat surface for 5 minutes; invert onto platter. Makes 6 servings.

FOR PERFECT CAKES EVERY TIME

Ingredients at Room Temperature

● Ingredients such as butter, eggs and milk should be at room temperature. Let butter stand for an hour or two or until softened. In a pinch, cube butter and soften on Low in microwave, or make your beater work a little harder.

● Warm milk to room temperature in microwave.

● To warm eggs to room temperature, place in bowl and cover with hot water. Let stand for about 5 minutes. This gives you time to measure out remaining ingredients.

Creaming Butter

● For butter cakes, the first step is to beat or "cream" the butter and sugar until very light and fluffy. Be patient with this step as the air that's beaten into this mixture will produce a finer, lighter cake.

Beating in Eggs

● Always beat in eggs one at a time.

Blending Dry Ingredients

● There are several ways to make sure that dry ingredients — flour, baking powder or baking soda, salt and spices — are well blended before mixing into the batter. Either sift them through a sifter or sieve into a bowl, or place them in a bowl and use a whisk to blend them thoroughly.

● If cocoa is one of these dry ingredients, you must sift or sieve the mixture to make sure that all the lumps have been broken down and that the cocoa is evenly distributed throughout the dry ingredients.

Adding Ingredients to Batter

● When adding dry and liquid ingredients to the batter, start and end with the dry, dividing the dry ingredients into three lots and the liquid into two. The divisions don't have to be exact — approximate is just fine.

● Use a wooden spoon or beater on low for this step and mix only long enough to blend the ingredients or your cake will be tough.

Soft Gingerbread

There's old-fashioned gingerbread flavor in every satisfying bite of this superlative cake. Serve when you want something pleasing without a lot of work. Add whipped cream or ice cream to slices of still-warm cake, if you wish.

1 cup	butter, softened	250 mL
1/2 cup	granulated sugar	125 mL
1	egg	1
1 cup	fancy molasses	250 mL
3 cups	all-purpose flour	750 mL
2 tsp	baking soda	10 mL
2 tsp	ginger	10 mL
1/2 tsp	cinnamon	2 mL
1/2 tsp	salt	2 mL
1/4 tsp	ground cloves	1 mL
1 cup	boiling water	250 mL

● In large bowl, beat butter with sugar until fluffy; beat in egg. Stir in molasses.

● Stir together flour, baking soda, ginger, cinnamon, salt and cloves. Add to molasses mixture alternately with water, making three additions of dry and two of water, stirring just until combined.

● Pour into greased 9-inch (2.5 L) square cake pan. Bake in 350°F (180°C) oven for 40 to 45 minutes or until cake tester inserted in center comes out clean. Let cool in pan on rack for 10 minutes. Cut into squares. Makes 10 servings.

TIP: Unless otherwise specified, choose fancy molasses for baking. "Fancy" is well marked on molasses bottles or cartons found in the baking section of supermarkets. Cooking or blackstrap molasses has a bitter edge that can spoil the flavor of baked goods unless prebalanced with other ingredients.

Cherry Chocolate Carrying Cake

3/4 cup	butter, softened	175 mL
1-1/2 cups	packed brown sugar	375 mL
4	eggs	4
1 tsp	vanilla	5 mL
1-3/4 cups	all-purpose flour	425 mL
1/2 cup	unsweetened cocoa powder	125 mL
2 tsp	baking powder	10 mL
1/2 tsp	salt	2 mL
1 cup	milk	250 mL
3 cups	pitted sour cherries (or 6 cups/1.5 L frozen cherries, drained and thawed)	750 mL
	TOPPING	
1/2 cup	packed brown sugar	125 mL
3 tbsp	all-purpose flour	50 mL
1/3 cup	butter	75 mL
	GLAZE	
2 oz	semisweet or white chocolate	60 g
2 tsp	butter	10 mL

● TOPPING: In bowl, stir sugar with flour; using pastry blender or two knives, cut in butter until crumbly. Set aside.

● In large bowl, beat butter with sugar until fluffy; beat in eggs, one at a time. Beat in vanilla. Sift together flour, cocoa, baking powder and salt; add to butter mixture alternately with milk, making three additions of dry and two of milk.

● Pour into greased and floured 13- x 9-inch (3.5 L) cake pan, smoothing top. Sprinkle with cherries, then topping. Bake in 350°F (180°C) oven for 40 to 45 minutes or until cake tester inserted in center comes out clean. Let cool in pan on rack.

● GLAZE: In top of double boiler over hot (not boiling) water, melt chocolate with butter; drizzle over cake. Makes 16 servings.

Summer family reunions, potluck suppers, car camping trips where you need something soothing to soften the edges of driving fatigue — all these occasions are perfect for this totable cake with the lusciousness of Black Forest cake but none of its fussiness.

Dark Chocolate Bundt Cake

3/4 cup	butter, softened	175 mL
1-1/2 cups	granulated sugar	375 mL
3 oz	unsweetened chocolate, melted	90 g
2	eggs	2
1 tsp	vanilla	5 mL
1-3/4 cups	all-purpose flour	425 mL
2 tsp	baking powder	10 mL
1/4 tsp	salt	1 mL
1 cup	milk	250 mL

● In bowl, beat butter with sugar until fluffy; stir in chocolate. Beat in eggs, one at a time. Beat in vanilla.

● Stir together flour, baking powder and salt; add to butter mixture alternately with milk, making three additions of dry and two of milk.

● Pour into greased and floured 10-inch (4 L) Bundt or tube pan, smoothing top. Bake in 350°F (180°C) oven for 50 minutes or until cake tester inserted in center comes out clean. Let cool in pan on rack for 10 minutes; turn out onto rack to cool completely. Makes 12 servings.

A chocolate cake like this dense, moist one is especially attractive with a dusting of icing sugar (see p. 58), or with a glaze.

GLAZING SNACKING CAKES

A glaze is both decorative and another way to add a touch of sweetness or a complementary flavor to snacking cakes.

● For this high chocolate cake, stir together 1 cup (250 mL) sifted icing sugar with 2 tbsp (25 mL) light cream and 1 tsp (5 mL) finely grated orange rind. Spoon over the cake so the glaze dips and drips over the sides. Lemon rind can replace the orange, and orange juice can replace the cream when a more intense citrus tang is appreciated.

Rhubarb Hazelnut Coffee Cake ▶

Spectacular is the only way to describe the look of this glossy rhubarb-topped coffee cake. Forced rhubarb, available from January to early April, is pinker than most garden stalks, but any rhubarb caps off this fine textured cake with aplomb.

1 cup	butter, softened	250 mL
1-1/3 cups	granulated sugar	325 mL
3	eggs	3
1 tsp	vanilla	5 mL
1/2 cup	plain yogurt	125 mL
2-1/3 cups	all-purpose flour	575 mL
1 tsp	baking powder	5 mL
1/2 tsp	cinnamon	2 mL
1/4 tsp	salt	1 mL
6 cups	chopped fresh rhubarb (about 1-3/4 lb/875 g)	1.5 L
	Chunky Rhubarb Sauce (recipe follows), optional	
	TOPPING	
1/2 cup	all-purpose flour	125 mL
1/4 cup	each granulated and packed brown sugar	50 mL
1/4 tsp	cinnamon	1 mL
1/4 cup	butter	50 mL
1/3 cup	hazelnuts, toasted and coarsely chopped (see box, p. 28)	75 mL

● In large bowl, beat butter with sugar until fluffy; beat in eggs, one at a time, beating well after each addition. Beat in vanilla, then yogurt.

● Stir together flour, baking powder, cinnamon and salt; stir into yogurt mixture. Pour into greased 13- x 9-inch (3.5 L) cake pan, smoothing top; sprinkle with rhubarb.

● TOPPING: In bowl, stir together flour, granulated and brown sugars and cinnamon. Using pastry blender or two knives, cut in butter until crumbly. Stir in hazelnuts. Sprinkle over rhubarb.

● Bake in 350°F (180°C) oven for about 1 hour or until cake tester inserted in center comes out clean. Let cool in pan on rack. Cut into squares. Serve with Chunky Rhubarb Sauce (if using). Makes 10 to 12 servings.

	CHUNKY RHUBARB SAUCE	
4 cups	chopped rhubarb (about 1-1/4 lb/625 g)	1 L
2/3 cup	granulated sugar	150 mL
1/2 cup	water	125 mL
4 tsp	cornstarch	20 mL
4 tsp	hazelnut liqueur or orange juice	20 mL

● In saucepan, bring rhubarb, sugar and water to boil over medium-high heat, stirring occasionally; reduce heat, cover and simmer for 3 minutes or until tender. Pressing gently on rhubarb, strain into bowl to make about 1-1/2 cups (375 mL) juice; set rhubarb aside. Return juice to saucepan.

● Dissolve cornstarch in liqueur; whisk into juice and cook over medium heat, whisking constantly, for 3 minutes or until thickened. Stir in any whole pieces of rhubarb. Serve warm or at room temperature. *(Sauce can be covered and refrigerated for up to 1 week.)* Makes 2 cups (500 mL).

JUST ADD A CUP OF COFFEE OR TEA

Anything sweet and baked tastes better with a cup of perfectly brewed coffee or tea.

● For coffee, the key ingredient is freshly roasted and freshly ground coffee, scrupulously clean equipment and accurate amounts of coffee and water according to your favorite method of brewing coffee. Count on 2 tbsp (25 mL) for each 3/4 cup (175 mL), increasing the amount for mugs, which can contain up to 1-1/2 cups.

● Black teas such as orange pekoe, Darjeeling and English and Irish Breakfast balance the sweet taste of cookies or cake, as does Earl Grey, the black tea scented with oil of bergamot. For a refreshing change, serve mint teas, teas from flowers or teas scented with lemon, orange or other fruits.

Sticky Almond Coffee Cake

A slice of indulgence to enjoy with caffe latte or cappuccino, morning or afternoon, summer deck or cosy fireside. Serve with melon wedges and berries in season, fresh pineapple or orange segments.

1/2 cup	butter, softened	125 mL
1 cup	granulated sugar	250 mL
2	eggs	2
1 tsp	almond extract	5 mL
2 cups	all-purpose flour	500 mL
1/3 cup	toasted ground almonds	75 mL
1 tsp	baking powder	5 mL
1/2 cup	milk	125 mL
1/3 cup	sliced almonds	75 mL

FILLING

1/3 cup	toasted ground almonds	75 mL
1/4 cup	all-purpose flour	50 mL
1/4 cup	packed brown sugar	50 mL
1/4 cup	butter	50 mL

TOPPING

1/2 cup	packed brown sugar	125 mL
2 tbsp	water	25 mL

● FILLING: In small bowl, combine almonds, flour and sugar. Using pastry blender or two knives, cut in butter until crumbly. Set aside.

● In large bowl, beat butter with sugar until fluffy. Beat in eggs, one at a time, beating well after each addition. Beat in almond extract. Stir together flour, ground almonds and baking powder; add to butter mixture alternately with milk, making three additions of dry and two of milk.

● Pour two-thirds of the batter into greased 8-1/2-inch (2.25 L) springform pan, smoothing top; scatter filling evenly over batter. Spread remaining batter smoothly over top; sprinkle with sliced almonds. Bake in 375°F (190°C) oven for about 1 hour or until cake tester inserted in center comes out clean. Let cool in pan on rack for 5 minutes.

● TOPPING: Meanwhile, in small saucepan, bring sugar and water to boil over medium-high heat; boil for 2 minutes or until thickened and syrupy. Pour evenly over cake. Remove side of pan; let cool. Makes 12 servings.

DRESSING UP A CAKE

Adding a Layered Filling

● Layer a cake before dusting with icing sugar or spreading with an icing (recipes, p. 45). Use a long serrated knife to cut cake horizontally in half. Carefully lift off top layer.

● Spread bottom layer with a preserve that complements the cake — cherry or raspberry jam for chocolate cakes, strawberry or apricot jam or lemon curd for white cakes, apple butter or marmalade for spice cakes. Replace top layer.

Dusting with Icing Sugar

● A dusting of icing sugar is one of the quickest and prettiest ways to dress up a cake. Either dust the top with this fine powdery sugar or create an attractive pattern on the cake by dusting the icing sugar through a doily or other cutout.

● To make your own pattern, cut out the appropriate shape — hearts for Valentine's Day, snowflakes for Christmas, maple leaves for Canada Day — in plain paper. Be sure to cut out as much pattern as possible since this is what will show on the cake.

● Layer the pattern over a completely cool cake. Hold sieve over cake and spoon icing sugar (about 2 tbsp/25 mL is usually enough) into the sieve. Shake gently over the entire cake to cover the cutout spaces thoroughly. Gently lift off paper.

The Elmwood Apple Cake

2-1/3 cups	granulated sugar	575 mL
2 tsp	cinnamon	10 mL
1 cup	vegetable oil	250 mL
4	eggs	4
1/2 cup	orange juice	125 mL
2 tbsp	vanilla	25 mL
3 cups	all-purpose flour	750 mL
1 tbsp	baking powder	15 mL
1/4 tsp	salt	1 mL
5	apples, peeled and chopped	5

● In small bowl, combine 1/3 cup (75 mL) of the sugar and cinnamon; set aside.

● In large bowl, beat together oil, eggs, remaining sugar, orange juice and vanilla. Combine flour, baking powder and salt; stir into egg mixture until smooth.

● Pour half of the batter into greased 10-inch (3 L) Bundt pan; arrange apples evenly over top. Sprinkle with half of the sugar mixture; pour remaining batter over top. Sprinkle with remaining sugar mixture.

● Bake in 350°F (180°C) oven for about 1 hour or until cake tester inserted in center comes out clean. *(Cake can be stored for up to 1 day.)* Makes 16 servings.

Carol MacDonald bakes this cinnamon-scented coffee cake for guests who meet for breakfast in the handsome Victorian dining room of the Elmwood, a delightful Charlottetown, PEI, bed-and-breakfast. Choose medium-sized apples for best results.

Terrific Cherry Upside-Down Cake

2 tbsp	packed brown sugar	25 mL
1 tbsp	butter, melted	15 mL
2 cups	pitted cherries	500 mL
1/4 cup	butter, softened	50 mL
1 cup	granulated sugar	250 mL
1	egg	1
1/2 tsp	almond extract	2 mL
1 cup	all-purpose flour	250 mL
1/2 cup	sliced almonds	125 mL
1 tsp	baking powder	5 mL
1/2 cup	buttermilk	125 mL

● In bowl, mix brown sugar with melted butter; add cherries and toss to coat. Spread in greased 8-inch (2 L) square cake pan. Set aside.

● In large bowl, beat butter with granulated sugar until fluffy; beat in egg and almond extract. Stir together flour, almonds and baking powder; stir half into butter mixture. Stir in buttermilk; stir in remaining flour mixture just until combined.

● Gently spoon over cherry mixture. Bake in 350°F (180°C) oven for 40 to 45 minutes or until cake tester inserted in center comes out clean. Let cool in pan on rack for 15 minutes. Run knife around edge of cake; invert onto platter. Makes 8 servings.

TIP: If using frozen cherries, let thaw in sieve set over a bowl. Press out excess juice before tossing cherries with butter and sugar. Add the cherry juice that remains in the bowl to any of your favorite morning juices, or bring to boil in small saucepan and boil for a few minutes or until syrupy. Brush over cherry layer on turned-out cake.

For cherry lovers everywhere, here's a delicious new way to enjoy this memorable fruit. Make this red-topped almond-studded cake in the summer with fresh juicy tart or sweet cherries —or skip the pitting and make it year-round with frozen. The tart red cherries frozen with 10% sugar (Montmorency) are recommended for their fine cherry taste and vivid color.

Cookies by the Jar

What can you hold deliciously in your hand, slip into a lunch, count on when you're hungry, munch on the run — and mix up quickly without fuss or fancy ingredients? Cookies, of course!

Jumbo Chocolate Chip Cookies ▶

For really indulgent chocolate chip cookies, use the jumbo-size chips, or chop solid chocolate into chunks. Milk chocolate can replace the semisweet chocolate.

1 cup	butter, softened	250 mL
3/4 cup	packed brown sugar	175 mL
3/4 cup	granulated sugar	175 mL
2	eggs	2
2 tsp	vanilla	10 mL
2-1/3 cups	all-purpose flour	575 mL
1 tsp	baking soda	5 mL
1 tsp	salt	5 mL
2 cups	coarsely chopped semisweet chocolate	500 mL
1 cup	coarsely chopped pecans or walnuts (optional)	250 mL

● In large bowl, beat butter with brown and granulated sugars; beat in eggs and vanilla. Combine flour, baking soda and salt; gradually stir into butter mixture. Stir in chocolate, and nuts (if using).

● Drop tablespoonfuls (15 mL) of dough, 2 inches (5 cm) apart, onto greased baking sheets. Bake in 375°F (190°C) oven for about 10 minutes or until golden brown around edges and soft in center. Makes 4 dozen cookies.

Crispy Almond Chip Cookies

Chunky with almonds and chocolate, these easy crispy cookies are sure to satisfy a craving for something sweet.

1 cup	butter, softened	250 mL
3/4 cup	packed brown sugar	175 mL
3/4 cup	granulated sugar	175 mL
1	egg	1
1/2 tsp	almond extract	2 mL
1 cup	all-purpose flour	250 mL
1 tsp	baking powder	5 mL
1/2 tsp	salt	2 mL
1/4 tsp	baking soda	1 mL
1 cup	quick-cooking rolled oats	250 mL
1 cup	chocolate chips	250 mL
3/4 cup	desiccated coconut	175 mL
3/4 cup	toasted chopped almonds (see box, p. 28)	175 mL

● In large bowl, beat butter with brown and granulated sugars; beat in egg and almond extract. Combine flour, baking powder, salt and baking soda; gradually stir into butter mixture. Stir in rolled oats, chocolate chips, coconut and almonds.

● Drop tablespoonfuls (15 mL) of dough onto greased baking sheets. With floured fork, flatten into 2-inch (5 cm) rounds. Bake in 375°F (190°C) oven for 10 minutes or until golden brown. Makes 4 dozen cookies.

Jumbo Chocolate Chip Cookies, Reverse Chocolate Chippers (p. 62) and Chocolate Orange Hazelnut Biscotti (p. 74)

Reverse Chocolate Chippers

White chocolate chips or chunks in a chewy, cocoa-rich dough are a delicious twist on a cookie classic (photo, p. 61).

1 cup	butter, softened	250 mL
2 cups	granulated sugar	500 mL
2	eggs	2
2 tsp	vanilla	10 mL
1-1/2 cups	all-purpose flour	375 mL
1 cup	unsweetened cocoa powder	250 mL
1 tsp	baking powder	5 mL
1 tsp	salt	5 mL
2 cups	white chocolate chunks	500 mL
3/4 cup	coarsely chopped toasted hazelnuts (see box, p. 28)	175 mL

● In large bowl, beat butter with sugar; beat in eggs and vanilla. Combine flour, cocoa, baking powder and salt; gradually stir into butter mixture. Stir in white chocolate and hazelnuts.

● Drop tablespoonfuls (15 mL) of dough, 2 inches (5 cm) apart, onto greased baking sheets. Bake in 350°F (180°C) oven for 12 minutes or until centers spring back when lightly touched. (Cookies will be soft but will firm up when cooled.) Makes 3 dozen cookies.

VARIATION

● DOUBLE CHOCOLATE MINT COOKIES: Substitute peppermint chips for white chocolate and 1 cup (250 mL) chopped pecans or walnuts for hazelnuts.

Peanut Butter-Chocolate Chip Cookies

Two all-time favorites make a winning combination in these nutty treats.

1/2 cup	butter, softened	125 mL
1 cup	granulated sugar	250 mL
1	egg	1
1 cup	chunky peanut butter	250 mL
1 tsp	vanilla	5 mL
1-1/4 cups	all-purpose flour	300 mL
1/2 tsp	baking powder	2 mL
1/2 tsp	baking soda	2 mL
1/2 tsp	salt	2 mL
1 cup	chocolate chips	250 mL
1/2 cup	chopped unsalted peanuts	125 mL

● In large bowl, beat butter with sugar; beat in egg, peanut butter and vanilla. Combine flour, baking powder, baking soda and salt; gradually stir into peanut butter mixture. Stir in chocolate chips and peanuts to make crumbly mixture.

● Shape dough into 1-1/2-inch (4 cm) balls; place balls, 3 inches (8 cm) apart, on greased baking sheets. With fingertips, flatten into 2-inch (5 cm) rounds. Bake in 350°F (180°C) oven for 15 minutes or until lightly browned. Makes 3 dozen cookies.

STORING COOKIES

● Let baked cookies cool completely on rack before storing.

● Store in airtight containers (tin, glass or plastic); cover with plastic wrap before closing with tight lids.

● Store crisp and soft cookies in separate containers.

● Store just one kind of cookie in a container, so flavors don't transfer.

● Store delicate cookies in layers between sheets of waxed paper.

● Store containers in cool place (not refrigerator).

FOR PERFECT COOKIES EVERY TIME

Getting Ready

- Preheat your oven and grease baking sheets with shortening or line with parchment paper before mixing the dough — unless there is a considerable time lag between preparing the cookie dough and baking the cookies.

- Opt for shiny baking sheets. Darker ones tend to overbrown the bottom of cookies before the cookie is baked through.

Measuring and Mixing Ingredients

- Use large eggs.

- Use an electric mixer to beat butter with sugar and to beat in eggs.

- Pack raisins, chopped dates or apricots, coconut or nuts lightly into dry measures to equal the measures in the book.

- Switch to a wooden spoon when adding dry ingredients and nuts, chocolate chips or coconut.

The Right Equipment

- **For drop cookies**, use an ordinary tableware teaspoon for smaller cookies, a soup or dessert spoon for larger cookies. The shallow bowl of these spoons, compared to the deepness of measuring spoons, makes it the easiest way to drop the cookies onto baking sheets.
- **For bars or squares**, use only the pan size specified. Spread the batter evenly to corners and sides of pan. Unless otherwise specified, set pan of baked bars on rack to cool completely before cutting.

From Bowl to Baking Sheet

- Always place dough on a cool baking sheet. A warm sheet will soften the dough and make it spread, resulting in thin, unevenly shaped cookies.

- Leave plenty of space between cookies when placing dough on sheets. Two to three inches (5 to 8 cm) is usually enough.

Baking the Cookies

- You'll get better cookies if you bake them one baking sheet at a time on rack positioned in middle of oven.

- If you must use two sheets, position them slightly above and slightly below the center and make sure that there are at least 2 inches (5 cm) between the edges of the baking sheet and the oven wall.

- Since many ovens heat irregularly, change the position of the baking sheets halfway through baking time, also turning sheets back to front.

Are They Done?

- Since baking times can only be approximate, check cookies at the minimum baking time. Most cookies are done when golden on the bottom and firm to the touch.

- Remove baking sheets from oven and let cookies firm up for a minute or two. Lift off with a flexible metal lifter and let cool on wire racks.

Canadian Living's Best Oatmeal Cookie Mix

This cookie maker's dream of a convenient mix makes enough for four batches of oven-fresh cookies — each just right for lunches, snacks and bake-sale requests. The mix comes with four delicious variations, but you may also want to mix up a batch or two using your favorite nuts or dried fruits.

4-1/2 cups	all-purpose flour	1.125 L
4-1/2 cups	quick-cooking rolled oats	1.125 L
4 cups	firmly packed brown sugar	1 L
1 tbsp	baking soda	15 mL
1 tbsp	baking powder	15 mL
2 tsp	salt	10 mL

● In large bowl, stir together flour, rolled oats, sugar, baking soda, baking powder and salt. Transfer to airtight container; store in cool, dry place for up to 2 months. Stir well before using. Makes 13 cups (3.25 L).

(clockwise from top right) Hermit, Oatmeal Toffee Crunch Cookie, two Oatmeal Raisin Cookies and Lemon Coconut Cookie

Oatmeal Cookies Five Ways

1/2 cup	butter, softened	125 mL
3-1/4 cups	Best Oatmeal Cookie Mix	800 mL
1	egg, beaten	1
4 tsp	water	20 mL
1 tsp	vanilla	5 mL

● In large bowl and using electric mixer at low speed, beat butter into Best Cookie Mix until blended. Stir in egg, water and vanilla until blended.

● Drop tablespoonfuls (15 mL) of dough onto greased baking sheets. Bake in 375°F (190°C) oven for about 10 minutes or until golden. Makes about 3 dozen cookies.

VARIATIONS

● OATMEAL TOFFEE CRUNCH COOKIES: Add 1 cup (250 mL) chopped milk-chocolate-covered-toffee bar, chocolate chips or peanut butter chips after beating butter into Mix.

● OATMEAL RAISIN COOKIES: Add 1 cup (250 mL) raisins and 1 tsp (5 mL) cinnamon after beating butter into Mix. Bake for 12 minutes.

● HERMITS: Omit vanilla. Add 1/2 cup (125 mL) each chopped candied fruit, walnuts and raisins, 1 tsp (5 mL) cinnamon, 1/2 tsp (2 mL) nutmeg and 1/4 tsp (1 mL) ground cloves after beating butter into Mix.

● LEMON COCONUT COOKIES: Omit vanilla. Add 1/2 cup (125 mL) shredded coconut and 2 tsp (10 mL) grated lemon rind after beating butter into Mix.

TIP: Refrigerating the spoonfuls of dough on baking sheets for 15 minutes before baking yields thicker, chewier cookies.

When it's time for a break, settle back with a cup of tea and luxuriate in the crisp buttery goodness of these simple cookies.

Crispy Oat Hermits

1-1/4 cups	shortening	300 mL
1-1/4 cups	packed brown sugar	300 mL
2	eggs	2
1 tsp	vanilla	5 mL
1-1/4 cups	all-purpose flour	300 mL
1 tsp	baking soda	5 mL
1 tsp	cinnamon	5 mL
1/2 tsp	salt	2 mL
1/2 tsp	ground cloves	2 mL
1/2 tsp	nutmeg	2 mL
2-1/2 cups	quick-cooking rolled oats	625 mL
1 cup	raisins	250 mL
1 cup	chopped dried apricots	250 mL
1 cup	chopped pecans or walnuts	250 mL

● In large bowl, beat shortening with sugar until fluffy; beat in eggs, one at a time. Beat in vanilla. Combine flour, baking soda, cinnamon, salt, cloves and nutmeg; gradually stir into butter mixture. Stir in rolled oats, raisins, apricots and nuts.

● Drop teaspoonfuls (5 mL) of dough onto greased baking sheets. Bake in 350°F (180°C) oven for 10 to 12 minutes or until golden. Makes 8 dozen cookies.

Share the fun of baking with kids and include lessons on measuring ingredients at the same time. Children can help by greasing or lining the baking sheets, cutting up fruit with scissors and dropping dough onto baking sheets.

No-Bake Peanut Butter Cookies

A no-bake cookie is a terrific way to introduce young children to the fun of making cookies.

1/2 cup	packed brown sugar	125 mL
1/2 cup	chunky peanut butter	125 mL
1/2 cup	corn syrup	125 mL
2 cups	cornflakes	500 mL

● In saucepan, heat brown sugar, peanut butter and corn syrup over medium heat, stirring constantly, just until sugar dissolves. Remove from heat; stir in cornflakes.

● Using 2 teaspoons, drop batter in mounds onto waxed paper, working quickly before mixture hardens. (If necessary, reheat gently just until soft enough to spoon.) Makes 3 dozen cookies.

Chocolate Oatmeal Fruit Drops

A tutti-frutti and chocolate combo will please kids and adults alike.

1 cup	butter, softened	250 mL
1 cup	packed brown sugar	250 mL
1/2 cup	granulated sugar	125 mL
1	egg	1
1 tsp	vanilla	5 mL
1/2 tsp	baking soda	2 mL
1/4 cup	boiling water	50 mL
2 cups	rolled oats	500 mL
1-1/2 cups	all-purpose flour	375 mL
1 tsp	salt	5 mL
1 cup	raisins	250 mL
1 cup	chopped candied mixed fruit	250 mL
1 cup	chocolate chips	250 mL

● In large bowl, beat butter with brown and granulated sugars; beat in egg and vanilla. Stir baking soda into boiling water until dissolved; stir into butter mixture.

● Combine rolled oats, flour and salt; gradually stir into butter mixture. Stir in raisins, candied fruit and chocolate chips.

● Drop heaping tablespoonfuls (15 mL) of dough, 2 inches (5 cm) apart, onto greased baking sheets; flatten slightly with fingertips or floured fork. Bake in 350°F (180°C) oven for about 15 minutes or until golden brown. Makes 4 dozen cookies.

Date Apricot Oatmeal Cookies

With dried fruit and rolled oats handy in the cupboard, these cookies are ready for baking any time you are. For a moister, chewier cookie, use dates packed in tubs rather than dates pressed into blocks.

1/2 cup	butter, softened	125 mL
1 cup	packed brown sugar	250 mL
1	egg	1
3 tbsp	vegetable oil	50 mL
2 tsp	vanilla	10 mL
1-1/2 cups	rolled oats	375 mL
1 cup	all-purpose flour	250 mL
1/2 tsp	baking powder	2 mL
1/2 tsp	baking soda	2 mL
1/4 tsp	salt	1 mL
1 cup	chopped dates	250 mL
1 cup	chopped dried apricots	250 mL
1 tsp	grated lemon rind	5 mL
1 tsp	lemon juice	5 mL

● In large bowl, beat butter with sugar; beat in egg, oil and vanilla. Combine rolled oats, flour, baking powder, baking soda and salt; gradually stir into butter mixture.

● Combine dates, apricots, lemon rind and juice; stir into butter mixture. Drop heaping tablespoonfuls (15 mL) of dough, 2 inches (5 cm) apart, onto greased baking sheets. Bake in 325°F (160°C) oven for 15 to 17 minutes or until golden brown. Makes 3-1/2 dozen cookies.

Peanut Butter Cookies ▲

1/2 cup	butter, softened	125 mL
1/2 cup	granulated sugar	125 mL
1/2 cup	packed brown sugar	125 mL
1	egg	1
1 cup	smooth peanut butter	250 mL
1/2 tsp	vanilla	2 mL
1-1/2 cups	all-purpose flour	375 mL
1/2 tsp	salt	2 mL
1/2 tsp	baking soda	2 mL
1 cup	unsalted peanuts	250 mL

● In large bowl, beat butter with granulated and brown sugars until fluffy; beat in egg, peanut butter and vanilla. Combine flour, salt and baking soda; gradually stir into peanut butter mixture. Stir in peanuts.

● Drop tablespoonfuls (15 mL) of dough, 1 inch (2.5 cm) apart, onto greased baking sheets; gently flatten with floured fork. Bake in 375°F (190°C) oven for 10 minutes or until light golden brown. Makes 3-1/2 dozen cookies.

There's something about the delicious aroma of freshly baked peanut butter cookies that lingers in our memory long after the last cookie has disappeared.

Shortbread Classics

Brown sugar in the shortbread is the secret behind these prizewinning cookies from Nora Clarke of Brantford, Ontario.

2 cups	butter, softened	500 mL
1 cup	packed light brown sugar, sifted	250 mL
3-1/2 cups	all-purpose flour	875 mL
1/2 cup	rice flour	125 mL
	Colored sprinkles (optional)	

- In large bowl, beat butter with sugar until fluffy. Sift together all-purpose and rice flours; gradually stir into butter mixture just until blended.
- Shape dough into disc; wrap and refrigerate for at least 1 hour or up to 1 day. Let soften slightly at room temperature before rolling, if too hard.
- Between waxed paper, roll out dough to 1/4-inch (5 mm) thickness. Using floured cookie cutters, cut out shapes. Sprinkle with colored sprinkles (if using).
- Bake on ungreased baking sheets in 275°F (140°C) oven for 25 to 30 minutes or until light golden around edges. Makes 5 dozen cookies.

Ginger Shortbread

Cookie Contest prizewinner Susan Ross of Waterford, Ontario, makes these ginger-studded cookies in the shape of dog bones — a perfect hostess gift when she and her miniature schnauzer, Sophie, do their round of Christmas visits!

1 cup	butter, softened	250 mL
1/2 cup	icing sugar, sifted	125 mL
3 tbsp	finely chopped candied ginger	50 mL
1/4 tsp	salt	1 mL
2 cups	all-purpose flour	500 mL

- In large bowl, beat butter with sugar until fluffy; beat in ginger and salt. Gradually stir in flour.
- Between waxed paper, roll out dough to 1/4-inch (5 mm) thickness. Using floured cookie cutters, cut out shapes.
- Bake on ungreased baking sheets in 300°F (150°C) oven for 17 to 20 minutes or until light golden around edges. Makes 5-1/2 dozen cookies.

ROLLING OUT COOKIES

- When rolling out delicate cookies such as shortbread, use a lightly floured pastry cloth and stockinette-covered rolling pin, or roll dough between two sheets of waxed paper.
- If using waxed paper, lift off top sheet of paper, replace over dough and carefully turn dough over. Remove the sheet that's now on top and cut out shapes. The cookies are easier to lift off the waxed paper if it has been previously peeled off.
- Monitor the temperature of cookies as you roll them. Too cold, and a buttery dough will crumble. Too warm and the dough softens and becomes sticky. Be prepared to rechill or let dough warm up, if necessary.
- Formed cookies such as shortbread keep their shape better if they are chilled before baking. Place filled baking sheets right in the refrigerator and let cookies firm up for 30 to 50 minutes before transferring to oven to bake.

FREEZING COOKIES

- Let cookies cool completely before packing. For safest keeping, arrange cookies in layers in airtight containers with rigid sides, separating layers with waxed paper, plastic wrap or foil. Cover the top with foil or plastic wrap and seal. Label and date container.
- To freeze bars and squares, it's a good idea to line the greased pan with foil so that when the bars have cooled and firmed up, the whole panful can be carefully lifted out, overwrapped with foil or plastic wrap and placed in airtight container to freeze. Or, overwrap the pan and place in airtight container.
- Frozen cookies thaw quickly. Remove from containers and arrange in single layer on serving plate where they will thaw, uncovered, at room temperature in about 15 minutes.

Lemon Poppy Seed Shortbread

3/4 cup	butter, softened	175 mL
1/2 cup	icing sugar	125 mL
3/4 cup	all-purpose flour	175 mL
1/2 cup	cornstarch	125 mL
1 tbsp	poppy seeds	15 mL
2 tsp	grated lemon rind	10 mL

- In large bowl, beat butter with sugar until fluffy. Combine flour, cornstarch, poppy seeds and lemon rind; gradually stir into butter mixture. Between waxed paper, press dough to 1-inch (2.5 cm) thickness; refrigerate for 20 minutes.
- On lightly floured surface, roll out dough to about 1/4-inch (5 mm) thickness. Using floured cookie cutters, cut out shapes. Press scraps together and repeat chilling and rolling once.
- Bake on lightly greased baking sheets in 300°F (150°C) oven for 10 minutes or until light golden around edges. Makes 3 dozen cookies.

TIP: A 2-inch (5 cm) round or shaped cookie cutter is ideal for shortbread.

Sweet and tangy, crunchy and crisp, these first-rate shortbread are worth making over and over again. Pair them with fresh summer berries, luscious peaches and nectarines, sorbets and ice creams.

Orange Shortbread

1 cup	butter, softened	250 mL
1/2 cup	(approx) granulated sugar	125 mL
2 tsp	dark rum	10 mL
1-1/2 cups	all-purpose flour	375 mL
2/3 cup	rice flour	150 mL
1/2 cup	chopped candied orange peel	125 mL

- In large bowl, beat butter with sugar until fluffy; beat in rum. Combine all-purpose and rice flours; gradually stir into butter mixture. Stir in orange peel. Gather dough into ball; lightly knead for about 1 minute or until smooth.
- On lightly floured surface or between waxed paper, roll out dough to 1/2-inch (1 cm) thickness. Using floured cookie cutter, cut out 2-inch (5 cm) rounds; place rounds, 1 inch (2.5 cm) apart, on ungreased baking sheets.
- Bake in 325°F (160°C) oven for 20 to 25 minutes or until light golden on bottoms and around edges; sprinkle with sugar. Makes 2 dozen cookies.

There's no need to restrict shortbread to the holiday season — these buttery cookies are wonderful all year long.

(from left) Christmas Ice Box Cookies, Chocolate Chow Mein Clusters and Orange Shortbread Cookies (p. 69)

Christmas Ice Box Cookies

1 cup	butter, softened	250 mL
1 cup	granulated sugar	250 mL
1 cup	packed brown sugar	250 mL
2	eggs	2
1 tbsp	grated lemon rind	15 mL
1 tsp	almond extract	5 mL
3 cups	all-purpose flour	750 mL
1 tsp	baking soda	5 mL
1 tsp	baking powder	5 mL
1/2 tsp	salt	2 mL
1/2 cup	each candied red and green cherries, halved	125 mL
1/2 cup	yellow candied pineapple chunks	125 mL
1/2 cup	chopped Brazil nuts	125 mL
1	egg white, lightly beaten	1
1 cup	sweetened flaked coconut	250 mL

● In large bowl, beat butter with granulated and brown sugars until fluffy; beat in eggs, one at a time. Beat in lemon rind and almond extract. Combine flour, baking soda, baking powder and salt; gradually stir into butter mixture. Stir in red and green cherries, pineapple and nuts; gather into ball.

● Divide dough in half; shape into 2 rolls about 11 inches (28 cm) long. Brush with egg white; roll in coconut to coat evenly. Wrap in plastic wrap and overwrap in foil; roll on work surface to shape log evenly. Refrigerate for at least 2 hours or until firm. *(Dough can be frozen for up to 1 month; let stand for 15 minutes before continuing with recipe.)*

● Cut each roll into 1/4-inch (5 mm) thick slices; place slices, 1 inch (2.5 cm) apart, on greased baking sheets. Bake in 350°F (180°C) oven for 10 to 12 minutes or until lightly golden around edges. Makes 6 dozen cookies.

It's great to have a few logs of this cookie dough on hand, ready to slice and bake into oven-fresh treats at a moment's notice.

Chocolate Chow Mein Clusters

1-1/2 cups	chocolate chips	375 mL
1 cup	butterscotch chips	250 mL
1/2 cup	butter	125 mL
1/4 cup	peanut butter	50 mL
2 cups	dry chow mein noodles	500 mL
1 cup	salted peanuts	250 mL
	Candied cherry halves	

● In top of double boiler over hot (not boiling) water, melt chocolate and butterscotch chips, butter and peanut butter, stirring often. In bowl, stir noodles with peanuts; pour in chocolate mixture and mix well.

● Spoon into 1-inch (2.5 cm) mounds on waxed paper-lined baking sheets; garnish each with cherry. Let stand for 30 minutes or refrigerate for 20 minutes or until firm. Makes 4 dozen clusters.

What is it about these crunchy cookies that makes them so addictive? Is it the way the chocolate coating melts so deliciously in your mouth? Is it because they're so quick and easy to make? Why not mix up a batch today and find out!

Almond Cookies

Judges of our recent Cookie Contest appreciated the deep almond flavor of this winning entry from Jean Keizer of Comox, British Columbia.

1 cup	butter, softened	250 mL
2 cups	packed brown sugar	500 mL
2	eggs	2
1 tsp	almond extract	5 mL
3-1/2 cups	all-purpose flour	875 mL
1 tsp	salt	5 mL
1 tsp	baking soda	5 mL
1 tsp	baking powder	5 mL
1	egg white, lightly beaten	1
1/2 cup	whole blanched almonds	125 mL
	FILLING	
1/4 cup	whole blanched almonds	50 mL
1/4 cup	granulated sugar	50 mL
1	egg yolk	1
1 tsp	lemon juice	5 mL
1/4 tsp	almond extract	1 mL

● In large bowl, beat butter with sugar until fluffy; beat in eggs, one at a time. Beat in almond extract. Combine flour, salt, baking soda and baking powder; gradually stir into butter mixture. Cover and refrigerate for at least 1 hour or until firm.

● FILLING: Meanwhile, in blender or food processor, grind almonds, sugar, egg yolk, lemon juice and almond extract until smooth.

● Roll heaping teaspoonfuls (5 mL) of dough into 1-inch (2.5 cm) balls. With finger, make indentation in center of each; spoon in about 1/4 tsp (1 mL) filling. Pinch off dime-size piece of dough; press over filling and reroll to seal and smooth edges.

● Place balls, 2 inches (5 cm) apart, on greased baking sheets. Brush tops with egg white; press almond lightly into each. Bake in 325°F (160°C) oven for 15 to 18 minutes or until light golden. Makes 5 dozen cookies.

Chocolate Macaroons

Macaroons are among the easiest cookies to make. These chocolate ones are particularly fine served with a selection of fruit sherbets or used as the base for a cookie sundae with your favorite ice cream and gooey chocolate sauce.

1 cup	granulated sugar	250 mL
1/3 cup	unsweetened cocoa powder	75 mL
3	egg whites	3
Pinch	salt	Pinch
2 cups	unsweetened desiccated coconut	500 mL
1 tsp	vanilla	5 mL

● Stir sugar with cocoa until smooth. In bowl, beat egg whites with salt until stiff peaks form. On low speed, gradually beat in sugar mixture, 1 heaping tbsp (15 mL) at a time; fold in coconut and vanilla.

● Drop teaspoonfuls (5 mL) of dough, 1 inch (2.5 cm) apart, onto greased baking sheets. Bake in 325°F (160°C) oven for 15 to 17 minutes or until outsides are dry but insides still soft. With spatula, immediately transfer to racks; let cool. Makes 4 dozen cookies.

Cherry Coconut Macaroons

3 cups	sweetened flaked coconut	750 mL
1/2 cup	all-purpose flour	125 mL
1/4 tsp	salt	1 mL
	Homemade Sweetened Condensed Milk (recipe follows)	
1 tsp	vanilla	5 mL
	Candied red and green cherry pieces	

● In bowl, combine coconut, flour and salt; stir in Homemade Sweetened Condensed Milk and vanilla.

● Drop heaping tablespoonfuls (15 mL) of dough, 1 inch (2.5 cm) apart, onto greased baking sheets; top each with candied cherry piece. Bake in 325°F (160°C) oven for 10 to 15 minutes or until golden brown around edges. Makes 2 dozen cookies.

	HOMEMADE SWEETENED CONDENSED MILK	
1 cup	skim milk powder	250 mL
2/3 cup	granulated sugar	150 mL
3 tbsp	butter	50 mL
1/3 cup	boiling water	75 mL

● In bowl, combine skim milk powder with sugar. Stir butter into boiling water until melted; pour into sugar mixture. Using electric mixer, beat for about 2 minutes or until smooth and creamy. Cover and refrigerate for 8 hours or until thickened. *(Milk can be refrigerated for up to 2 weeks.)* Makes 1-1/4 cups (300 mL).

These chewy, cherry-dappled macaroons are wonderful for Christmas and for cookie exchanges. If you're short of time, substitute one can (300 mL) sweetened condensed milk for the homemade.

Lemon Hazelnut Biscotti Bars

1-1/2 cups	all-purpose flour	375 mL
1/4 cup	toasted hazelnuts, coarsely chopped (see box, p. 28)	50 mL
2 tsp	baking powder	10 mL
2/3 cup	granulated sugar	150 mL
2	egg whites	2
1	egg	1
1/3 cup	butter, melted	75 mL
1 tbsp	grated lemon rind	15 mL
2 tsp	vanilla	10 mL

● In large bowl, combine flour, hazelnuts and baking powder; set aside.

● Reserve 1 tsp (5 mL) of the sugar. Whisk together 1 of the egg whites, egg, remaining sugar, butter, lemon rind and vanilla; stir into flour mixture.

● Pat dough into greased 9-inch (2.5 L) square cake pan. Brush with some of the remaining egg white; sprinkle with reserved sugar. Bake in 350°F (180°C) oven for 30 minutes.

● Cut into 24 bars; separate bars and arrange on ungreased baking sheet. Bake for 15 to 20 minutes or until crisp and golden. Makes 2 dozen bars.

Lighter and lower-fat is a trend that affects even cookies, a baked item that depends on sweetness and butteriness for its appeal. Rather than ruin a good cookie by reducing the ingredients that make it good, look to a cookie that's naturally lower in fat. Case in point — biscotti, a crunchy lighter cookie that still delivers full flavor and satisfaction.

Chocolate Orange Hazelnut Biscotti

There's always a buzz in coffee shops — customers lining up for a cappuccino, latte (espresso with lots of milk) or machiatto (espresso stained with a dash of milk). Part of the chic atmosphere in these cafés is the big glass jars of finger-shaped biscotti — richer and more luxurious than they ever were in Italy. The combination of chocolate, hazelnut, orange and coffee flavors in these particular biscotti makes them one of the more indulgent cookies to dip into all kinds of coffee. (Photo, p. 61.)

1 tbsp	instant coffee granules	15 mL
2 tsp	vanilla	10 mL
1-1/2 cups	all-purpose flour	375 mL
1/2 cup	unsweetened cocoa powder	125 mL
1/2 cup	hazelnuts, toasted (see box, p. 28)	125 mL
1/3 cup	chocolate chips	75 mL
2 tsp	baking powder	10 mL
2	eggs	2
3/4 cup	granulated sugar	175 mL
1/3 cup	butter, melted	75 mL
1 tbsp	grated orange rind	15 mL
1	egg white, lightly beaten	1

- In small bowl, dissolve coffee granules in vanilla; set aside.
- In large bowl, combine flour, cocoa, hazelnuts, chocolate chips and baking powder. Whisk together eggs, sugar, butter, orange rind and coffee mixture; stir into flour mixture to form soft dough.
- On lightly floured surface, gently press dough into smooth ball. Divide in half; roll each into 12-inch (30 cm) long log. Transfer to ungreased baking sheet; brush tops with egg white. Bake in 350°F (180°C) oven for 20 minutes; let cool for 5 minutes. Transfer carefully to cutting board.
- Slice each log diagonally into 3/4-inch (2 cm) thick slices; stand slices upright on baking sheet. Bake for 25 minutes longer; remove from pan to racks and let cool. *(Biscotti can be layered between waxed paper and stored in airtight container for up to 2 weeks.)* Makes 2 dozen biscotti.

Baci di Dama ▶

One taste of these delicate almond wafers, sandwiched together with melted chocolate, and you'll understand why the Italians call them "lady's kisses." Resist no more!

2/3 cup	butter, softened	175 mL
1 cup	granulated sugar	250 mL
1-1/2 tsp	finely grated lemon rind	7 mL
1 tsp	vanilla	5 mL
1 cup	ground almonds	250 mL
1 cup	all-purpose flour	250 mL
3 oz	semisweet chocolate, coarsely chopped	90 g

- In bowl, beat together butter, sugar, lemon rind and vanilla until very light. Beat in almonds; beat in flour to make crumbly mixture. Lightly squeeze dough into ball.
- Shape level teaspoonfuls (5 mL) of dough into balls. Place about 1-1/2 inches (4 cm) apart on parchment-paper-lined or lightly greased baking sheets; flatten slightly with palm. Bake in 350°F (180°C) oven for 12 to 15 minutes or just until lightly golden. Let cool completely on baking sheets on rack.
- Meanwhile, in top of double boiler over hot (not boiling) water, melt chocolate. Spread over underside of one of the cookies; sandwich with another cookie. Repeat with remaining cookies. Makes 4 dozen cookies.

(clockwise from left) Baci di Dama, Toffee Cookie Brittle (p. 84) and Butterscotch Walnut Bars (p. 84)

Hamantaschen ◀

2/3 cup	butter, softened	150 mL
1 cup	granulated sugar	250 mL
3	eggs	3
3 tbsp	liquid honey	45 mL
1 tsp	vanilla	5 mL
3 cups	all-purpose flour	750 mL
1 tsp	baking powder	5 mL
	FILLING	
2 cups	pitted prunes	500 mL
1 cup	raisins	250 mL
1/2 cup	walnuts	125 mL
1 tsp	grated lemon rind	5 mL
1/4 cup	lemon juice	50 mL
2 tbsp	granulated sugar	25 mL
1	egg, lightly beaten	1

- In large bowl, beat butter with sugar until fluffy; beat in eggs, one at a time. Beat in honey and vanilla. Combine flour with baking powder; gradually stir into butter mixture. Press gently into ball; wrap and refrigerate for at least 2 hours or up to 3 days.
- FILLING: In food processor, finely chop together prunes, raisins, walnuts, lemon rind and juice and sugar.
- On lightly floured surface, roll out dough, one-quarter at a time, to 1/8-inch (3 mm) thickness. Using floured 2-1/2-inch (6 cm) round cookie cutter, cut out rounds. Place heaping teaspoonful (5 mL) filling in center of each. Fold three sides up to make three corners; pinch each corner to seal. Reroll scraps once.
- Place on greased baking sheets; brush egg over edges. Bake in 350°F (180°C) oven for 15 to 20 minutes or until golden. Makes 5 dozen cookies.

Tricornered hat-shaped hamantaschen, filled with dried fruit, poppy seeds or jam, are a much anticipated treat during Purim, one of the liveliest of the Jewish holidays.

Lemon Almond Bars

3/4 cup	butter, softened	175 mL
1/2 cup	granulated sugar	125 mL
1/4 tsp	salt	1 mL
2 cups	all-purpose flour	500 mL
	TOPPING	
4	eggs	4
1-1/2 cups	granulated sugar	375 mL
1/4 cup	all-purpose flour	50 mL
2 tbsp	grated lemon rind	25 mL
1/3 cup	lemon juice	75 mL
1-1/2 cups	sliced almonds	375 mL

- In bowl, beat together butter, sugar and salt until fluffy; stir in flour until combined. Press into ungreased 13- x 9-inch (3.5 L) cake pan. Bake in 325°F (160°C) oven for about 35 minutes or until golden.
- TOPPING: In bowl, whisk together eggs, sugar, flour, lemon rind and juice until smooth; pour over base. Sprinkle with almonds. Bake for 20 to 25 minutes or until set. Let cool on rack; cut into bars. Makes 30 bars.

One of the finest of the shortbread-topped pan cookies, these lemony bars beg for a glass of iced tea and a verandah to rock away a summer's afternoon. Because the bars are so wonderfully rich, they make the leap from casual to special-occasion in delicious style.

Dutch Butter Bars ▲

Make merry with Dutch-Canadians who celebrate St. Nicholas Day (December 6) by making up a batch of almond shortbread-like bars — known in Dutch as boterkoek.

2/3 cup	butter, softened	150 mL
1 cup	granulated sugar	250 mL
1	egg	1
1 tsp	almond extract	5 mL
1-1/2 cups	all-purpose flour	375 mL
1/2 tsp	baking powder	2 mL
	TOPPING	
1	egg	1
1 tbsp	milk	15 mL
	Sliced almonds	

● In bowl, beat butter with sugar until fluffy. Beat in egg and almond extract. Combine flour with baking powder; stir into butter mixture until smooth. Spread in greased 8-inch (2 L) square cake pan.

● TOPPING: Beat egg with milk; brush over dough. Top with almonds. Bake in 350°F (180°C) oven for 30 minutes or until golden brown. Let cool on rack; cut into bars. Makes 16 bars.

Peanut Butter Squares

2/3 cup	corn syrup	150 mL
1/2 cup	smooth peanut butter	125 mL
4 cups	crispy rice cereal	1 L
1/2 cup	raisins	125 mL

● In large saucepan, heat corn syrup and peanut butter over medium heat until melted. Stir in rice cereal and raisins until coated.

● Spread in lightly greased 8-inch (2 L) square baking dish. Refrigerate for about 1 hour or until firm. Cut into squares. Makes 16 squares.

Peanut butter adds its appeal to crispy rice squares. These are good starter cookies for fledgling cooks.

Fruit and Nut Bars

1 cup	finely chopped dates	250 mL
1 cup	raisins	250 mL
1 cup	mixed candied fruit	250 mL
1/4 cup	rum	50 mL
1 cup	chopped pecans or walnuts	250 mL
1 cup	all-purpose flour	250 mL
1/2 cup	butter, softened	125 mL
1 cup	packed brown sugar	250 mL
2	eggs	2
1 tsp	vanilla	5 mL
1/2 tsp	baking powder	2 mL
1/4 tsp	each cinnamon, nutmeg, allspice and salt	1 mL

● In bowl, combine dates, raisins, candied fruit and rum; let stand for 2 hours, stirring occasionally. Add nuts and 1/4 cup (50 mL) of the flour, tossing to coat.

● In large bowl, beat butter with sugar until fluffy; beat in eggs and vanilla. Combine remaining flour, baking powder, cinnamon, nutmeg, allspice and salt; stir into batter. Stir in floured fruit and nuts.

● Line 9-inch (2.5 L) square cake pan with greased waxed paper; spoon in batter, spreading evenly. Bake in 350°F (180°C) oven for 40 minutes or until tester inserted in center comes out clean. Let cool in pan on rack. Remove from pan in one piece. Wrap in plastic wrap or foil; let stand for 3 days before cutting into bars. Makes 40 bars.

These bars are like memories of fruitcake, and will appeal to anyone who enjoys the spicy fruit and nut flavors but doesn't have the time to make a dense fruitcake.

Power Bars

2 cups	whole wheat flour	500 mL
1/2 cup	packed brown sugar	125 mL
1/4 cup	skim milk powder	50 mL
1/4 cup	wheat germ	50 mL
1 tsp	baking powder	5 mL
1-1/2 cups	raisins or chopped dried apricots	375 mL
1/2 cup	unsalted sunflower seeds	125 mL
2	eggs	2
1/2 cup	vegetable oil	125 mL
1/2 cup	molasses	125 mL
1/3 cup	peanut butter	75 mL

● In bowl, combine flour, sugar, skim milk powder, wheat germ and baking powder; stir in raisins and sunflower seeds. Whisk together eggs, oil, molasses and peanut butter; stir into dry ingredients until blended.

● Spread in greased 9-inch (2.5 L) square cake pan. Bake in 350°F (180°C) oven for 35 minutes or until browned and firm to the touch. Let cool on rack; cut into bars. Makes 24 bars.

For anyone who packs lunch bags or needs inspiration for make-ahead totable treats for summer holiday drives — this bar is for you!

Soft Granola Bars

Appealingly sweet and chock-full of oats, these energy-packed bars are a great pick-me-up during a busy day.

3 cups	quick-cooking rolled oats	750 mL
1/2 cup	packed brown sugar	125 mL
1/4 cup	wheat germ	50 mL
1/2 cup	butter	125 mL
1/4 cup	corn syrup	50 mL
1/4 cup	liquid honey	50 mL
1/2 cup	chocolate chips	125 mL
1/2 cup	flaked coconut	125 mL

● In bowl, combine rolled oats, sugar and wheat germ. Using pastry blender or two knives, cut in butter until crumbly. Stir in corn syrup and honey until combined. Stir in chocolate chips and coconut.

● Press into greased 9-inch (2.5 L) square cake pan. Bake in 350°F (180°C) oven for 20 to 25 minutes or until golden. Let cool on rack for 10 minutes; cut into bars. Makes 15 bars.

Oatmeal Squares Four Ways

It all started with date squares — a butter-and-rolled-oats base and topping separated by a thick date and orange filling. Then creative cooks got inspired by different fillings — raisins, cranberries and mincemeat. The result? A variety of old-fashioned squares that date back decades and are predictably going to be just as popular in decades to come.

2 cups	rolled oats	500 mL
2 cups	all-purpose flour	500 mL
1 cup	packed brown sugar	250 mL
1 tsp	baking powder	5 mL
1/4 tsp	salt	1 mL
1 cup	butter, melted	250 mL
	DATE FILLING	
3 cups	chopped dates (1 lb/500 g)	750 mL
1/2 cup	packed brown sugar	125 mL
1 cup	water	250 mL
1 tbsp	coarsely grated lemon rind	15 mL
2 tbsp	lemon juice	25 mL

● DATE FILLING: In saucepan on top of stove, stir together dates, sugar, water, lemon rind and juice; cover and cook over medium heat, stirring occasionally, for about 8 minutes or until thickened. Let cool.

● In large bowl, stir together rolled oats, flour, sugar, baking powder and salt, blending well. Drizzle with butter, tossing to make moist crumbly mixture. Pat half into greased 9-inch (2.5 L) square cake pan. Spoon in date filling, spreading evenly; sprinkle with remaining rolled oats mixture.

● Bake in 350°F (180°C) oven for 30 to 35 minutes or until topping is golden brown. Let cool in pan on rack; cut into squares. Makes 16 large squares.

VARIATIONS

● APPLE MINCEMEAT SQUARES: Replace date filling with 3 cups (750 mL) mincemeat combined with 1 cup (250 mL) diced peeled apples and 1 tbsp (15 mL) coarsely grated orange rind (optional).

● RASPBERRY ALMOND SQUARES: Replace date filling with 2 cups (500 mL) raspberry jam (preferably light extra fruit jam) combined with 1/2 cup (125 mL) slivered almonds.

● CRANBERRY ORANGE SQUARES: Replace date filling with 3 cups (750 mL) whole berry cranberry sauce combined with 1 tbsp (15 mL) coarsely grated orange rind.

ZESTERS ARE HANDY

A zester makes quick work of removing the thin outer yellow layer of lemon peel or the orange layer of orange peel. It can also replace the fine side of a box grater when coarsely grated rind is required. This handy tool, with five little holes punched in the end of the blade, is sold wherever kitchen gadgets are available. Drawn firmly across the skin of an orange or lemon, the zester pares off fine strips of the zest but none of the bitter pith.

Flake-and-Fruit Squares

3 cups	cornflakes	750 mL
1/2 cup	sunflower seeds	125 mL
1/2 cup	whole unblanched almonds	125 mL
1/4 cup	sesame seeds	50 mL
1/4 cup	chopped dried dates	50 mL
1/4 cup	chopped dried apricots	50 mL
1/4 cup	butter	50 mL
3 cups	miniature marshmallows	750 mL
1 tsp	vanilla	5 mL

- In large bowl, combine cornflakes, sunflower seeds, almonds, sesame seeds, dates and apricots.
- In large saucepan, melt butter over low heat; add marshmallows and cook, stirring constantly, until melted. Stir in vanilla. Stir into cornflake mixture until well blended.
- Spoon into greased foil-lined 9-inch (2.5 L) square cake pan, packing firmly. Refrigerate for about 1 hour or until set. Remove from pan; cut into squares. Makes 16 squares.

If you think that crispy rice is the only cereal you can use in squares, check out the bold new flavor that cornflakes give!

Microwave Peanut and Chocolate Squares ▼

These popular squares are so easy that kids can make them themselves. Wrap extras and tuck them into lunches.

2 cups	quick-cooking rolled oats	500 mL
1/3 cup	packed brown sugar	75 mL
1/4 cup	chocolate chips or raisins	50 mL
1	egg	1
1/4 cup	corn syrup	50 mL
1/4 cup	peanut butter	50 mL
1-1/2 tsp	vanilla	7 mL

- In bowl, combine rolled oats, brown sugar and chocolate chips. In separate bowl, stir together egg, corn syrup, peanut butter and vanilla; stir into oats mixture until evenly coated.
- With greased fingertips, pat mixture evenly into greased 8-inch (2 L) square microwaveable dish. Microwave at High for 6 minutes, rotating every two minutes. Let cool on rack for 10 minutes; cut into squares. Makes 16 squares.

Chocolate Chip Blondies

One bite of these satisfying bars and you'll wonder how anything so delicious can be so easy, too — just mix, spread in the pan and bake.

1/2 cup	butter, softened	125 mL
1 cup	packed brown sugar	250 mL
1	egg	1
1 tsp	vanilla	5 mL
1 cup	all-purpose flour	250 mL
1 tsp	baking powder	5 mL
1/4 tsp	salt	1 mL
1/2 cup	chocolate chips	125 mL
1/2 cup	chopped walnuts	125 mL

- In bowl, beat butter with sugar until fluffy; beat in egg and vanilla. Combine flour, baking powder and salt; stir into butter mixture until blended. Stir in chocolate chips and walnuts.
- Spread in greased 8-inch (2 L) square cake pan. Bake in 350°F (180°C) oven for about 25 minutes or until golden. Let cool on rack; cut into squares. Makes 12 squares.

Chocolate Caramel Brownies ▶

These luxurious brownies make a sensational dessert served with ice cream and Brandied Chocolate Sauce.

1 cup	butter, cubed	250 mL
4 oz	unsweetened chocolate, chopped	125 g
1-3/4 cups	granulated sugar	425 mL
4	eggs, beaten	4
1 tsp	vanilla	5 mL
1-1/4 cups	all-purpose flour	300 mL
1/2 tsp	salt	2 mL
	TOPPING	
1/2 cup	whipping cream	125 mL
1/2 cup	packed brown sugar	125 mL
1/4 cup	butter	50 mL
1-1/2 cups	pecan halves	375 mL
1 cup	chocolate chips	250 mL
	Brandied Chocolate Sauce (recipe follows)	

- In top of double boiler over hot (not boiling) water, melt butter with chocolate; remove from heat. Whisk in sugar until well combined. Gradually stir in eggs and vanilla. Gradually stir in flour and salt.
- Pour into greased 13- x 9-inch (3.5 L) cake pan; bake in 400°F (200°C) oven for 12 minutes. (Batter will not be totally cooked but will be set enough to add topping.)
- TOPPING: Meanwhile, in saucepan, bring cream, sugar and butter to boil; boil for 3 minutes. Sprinkle brownies with pecans; drizzle evenly with cream mixture. Bake for 8 to 10 minutes or until golden but not browned.
- Sprinkle brownies with chocolate chips; let stand until melted slightly. Swirl with knife to let some topping show through. Let cool on rack; cut into squares. Serve with Brandied Chocolate Sauce. Makes 16 squares.

	BRANDIED CHOCOLATE SAUCE	
1/2 cup	whipping cream	125 mL
5 oz	semisweet chocolate, chopped	150 g
1 tbsp	butter	15 mL
2 tsp	brandy or nut liqueur	10 mL

- In small saucepan, bring cream to boil; remove from heat. Whisk in chocolate until melted. Whisk in butter and brandy. Let cool slightly before serving. *(Sauce can be covered and refrigerated for up to 1 week; reheat gently to serve.)* Makes 1 cup (250 mL).

Butterscotch Walnut Bars

Choose any kind of nut you like for these toothsome bars. For a special touch, dip the tines of a fork into melted chocolate and flick over the surface to make a pretty pattern. (Photo, p. 75.)

1 cup	packed brown sugar	250 mL
1/4 cup	butter	50 mL
1	egg	1
1 tsp	vanilla (or 1/4 tsp/1 mL maple extract)	5 mL
1/2 cup	all-purpose flour	125 mL
1/4 tsp	baking soda	1 mL
1/4 tsp	salt	1 mL
1-1/2 cups	walnut halves	375 mL

- In saucepan, cook brown sugar and butter over medium heat, stirring, just until melted. Let cool slightly; beat in egg and vanilla.
- Combine flour, baking soda and salt; stir into sugar mixture just until blended. Stir in walnuts.
- Spread in greased 8-inch (2 L) square cake pan. Bake in 350°F (180°C) oven for 15 to 18 minutes or until golden brown and set. Let cool in pan on rack for 15 minutes; cut into bars. Makes 12 bars.

Hello Dolly Bars

You'll be excused if you think these squares are really candy. Like many squares, Hello Dolly has tilted to pure confection. But, every once in a while, why not enjoy a tiny mouthful in all its glory of coconut, butterscotch, chocolate and pecans.

2 cups	graham cracker crumbs	500 mL
1/2 cup	butter, melted	125 mL
1 cup	each semisweet chocolate and butterscotch chips	250 mL
1-1/2 cups	chopped pecans	375 mL
1 cup	unsweetened shredded or desiccated coconut	250 mL
1	can (300 mL) sweetened condensed milk (see p. 73)	1

- In bowl, stir graham cracker crumbs with butter until well moistened. Pat evenly into lightly greased 13- x 9-inch (3 L) baking dish.
- Scatter chocolate and butterscotch chips evenly over base. Sprinkle with pecans, then coconut. Drizzle condensed milk evenly over top.
- Bake in 350°F (180°C) oven for about 30 minutes or until golden. Let cool completely in pan on rack; cut into squares. Makes 30 small squares.

Toffee Cookie Brittle

Once this sheet of baked cookie dough, chunky with pieces of chocolate-covered toffee bars, is broken into pieces like brittle, it will disappear like magic — so be sure you help yourself to a few pieces first! For our photo (p. 75), we cut the dough into large triangles.

1-1/4 cups	butter, softened	300 mL
1-1/2 cups	granulated sugar	375 mL
1-1/2 tsp	vanilla	7 mL
1/2 tsp	salt	2 mL
3 cups	all-purpose flour	750 mL
1 cup	chocolate chips	250 mL
6	bars (each 39 g) milk-chocolate-covered toffee, chopped	6

- In bowl, beat butter with sugar until fluffy; beat in vanilla and salt. Gradually stir in flour until combined. Stir in chocolate chips and chopped candy bars.
- Gently squeeze handfuls of dough just until mixture holds together; pat evenly into ungreased 17- x 11-inch (45 x 28 cm) jelly roll pan. Bake in 325°F (160°C) oven for about 30 minutes or until just firm to the touch. Let cool in pan on rack; break into pieces. Makes 6 dozen pieces.

Butter Tart Pecan Squares

2 cups	all-purpose flour	500 mL
2 tbsp	granulated sugar	25 mL
1 cup	butter, cubed	250 mL
	FILLING	
3	eggs	3
2-1/4 cups	packed brown sugar	550 mL
3/4 cup	butter, melted	175 mL
1 tbsp	vinegar	15 mL
1-1/2 tsp	vanilla	7 mL
1-1/2 cups	currants or raisins	375 mL
1/2 cup	chopped pecans	125 mL
	Icing sugar	

● In bowl, stir flour with sugar. Using pastry blender or two knives, cut in butter until crumbly. Press into 13- x 9-inch (3.5 L) cake pan. Bake in 350°F (180°C) oven for 20 to 25 minutes or until set.

● FILLING: In bowl, whisk eggs with sugar; whisk in butter, vinegar and vanilla. Stir in currants and pecans; pour over base.

● Bake, shielding edges with foil, if necessary, to prevent overbrowning, for 30 to 40 minutes or until golden brown and slightly firm to the touch. Let cool in pan on rack. Cover and let stand overnight; cut into squares. Sift icing sugar over top. Makes 35 squares.

If sweet and rich describe your preference in squares, then these Cookie Contest prizewinners from Arlene Bennett of Cape Breton, Nova Scotia, are your ticket to satisfaction.

Chocolate Candy Buttercrunch

50	unsalted soda crackers	50
1 cup	unsalted butter	250 mL
1 cup	packed brown sugar	250 mL
6 oz	semisweet chocolate, coarsely chopped	175 g

● Line bottom and sides of 15- x 11-inch (38 x 28 cm) jelly roll pan with foil; line bottom with parchment paper. Arrange soda crackers in pan, breaking pieces to fit if necessary.

● In saucepan, bring butter and sugar to boil over medium-high heat, stirring constantly with wooden spoon and reducing heat to medium if mixture starts to stick to bottom. Boil for 3 minutes, stirring constantly. Pour over crackers.

● Bake in 350°F (180°C) oven for about 15 minutes or until browned and bubbling. Remove from oven; sprinkle chocolate over top. Let stand on rack for 5 minutes; run tines of fork over top to decorate. Cut into squares or break into small pieces. Refrigerate for at least 1 hour or up to 2 days. Makes about 6 dozen pieces.

These cookies are so easy to make, you won't believe how good they taste. For Passover, replace soda crackers with four sheets regular matzo and use margarine instead of butter.

CHOCOLATE GINGER BARS

This sophisticated no-bake bar marries the wonderful tastes of chocolate with ginger.

● In saucepan, melt together 1/3 cup (75 mL) butter, 8 oz (250 g) semisweet chocolate and 3 tbsp (50 mL) corn syrup over low heat.

● In food processor, chop 8 oz (250 g) ginger cookies to make coarse crumbs; stir into chocolate mixture along with 2 tbsp (25 mL) chopped crystalized ginger.

● Spread in greased 8-inch (2 L) square cake pan; refrigerate for 2 hours. Cut into squares; dust with icing sugar. Makes 20 squares.

Peanut Butter Brownies

Inspired by Canadian-grown peanuts, these brownies offer yet another very munchable variation on the theme of crunchy peanuts and ever-popular chocolate.

3/4 cup	butter, softened	175 mL
3/4 cup	peanut butter	175 mL
2 cups	packed brown sugar	500 mL
3	eggs	3
1 tsp	vanilla	5 mL
1-3/4 cups	all-purpose flour	425 mL
1/4 cup	unsweetened cocoa powder	50 mL
2 tsp	baking powder	10 mL
1/2 tsp	salt	2 mL
1-1/2 cups	peanuts	375 mL
1-1/2 cups	chocolate chips	375 mL

● In large bowl, beat together butter, peanut butter and sugar until fluffy; beat in eggs, one at a time. Beat in vanilla. Sift together flour, cocoa, baking powder and salt; stir all at once into butter mixture.

● Spread in greased 13- x 9-inch (3.5 L) cake pan, smoothing top. Sprinkle with peanuts; press firmly into batter. Bake in 350°F (180°C) oven for about 25 minutes or until sides begin to pull away from pan.

● Sprinkle chocolate chips over brownies; let stand until melted. Run tines of fork over top to decorate. Let cool on rack; cut into squares. Makes 32 brownies.

Truffle Brownies

Here's all the dense, chocolatey flavor of truffles in a quick and easy pan brownie. To enjoy these during Passover, simply replace the flour with matzo cake meal and use margarine instead of butter.

1 cup	butter	250 mL
2 cups	packed brown sugar	500 mL
1 cup	all-purpose flour	250 mL
3/4 cup	unsweetened cocoa powder, sifted	175 mL
1/2 cup	finely chopped toasted walnuts (see box, p. 28)	125 mL
3	eggs	3
2 tsp	vanilla	10 mL
	GLOSSY FUDGE ICING	
8 oz	semisweet chocolate	250 g
1/2 cup	strong coffee	125 mL
2 tbsp	butter, softened	25 mL

● In small saucepan, melt butter over low heat; let cool to room temperature. Whisk in brown sugar, flour, cocoa, walnuts, eggs and vanilla.

● Spread in greased 11- x 7-inch (2 L) baking dish; bake in 350°F (180°C) oven for about 25 minutes or just until set and top is dry to the touch. Let cool completely on rack.

● GLOSSY FUDGE ICING: Chop chocolate coarsely; place in bowl. Bring coffee to boil; pour over chocolate, stirring until melted. Refrigerate for 15 minutes. Whisk in butter; spread over brownies. Run tines of fork over top to decorate. Refrigerate for at least 8 hours or up to 12 hours. Cut into squares. Makes 30 small brownies.

Brownie Sundae Heart

1 cup	all-purpose flour	250 mL
1/2 cup	granulated sugar	125 mL
1/2 cup	unsweetened cocoa powder	125 mL
1/3 cup	slightly softened butter, cubed	75 mL
1	egg	1
	BROWNIE FILLING	
3 oz	each unsweetened and semisweet chocolate, coarsely chopped	90 g
1/2 cup	butter, cubed	125 mL
1-1/2 cups	granulated sugar	375 mL
2 tsp	vanilla	10 mL
3	eggs	3
3/4 cup	all-purpose flour	175 mL
4	bars (each 55 g) milk-chocolate-covered toffee, coarsely chopped	4
	TOPPING	
4 cups	vanilla ice cream	1 L
2 oz	semisweet chocolate, chopped	60 g
1/4 cup	whipping cream	50 mL

● In food processor, mix flour, sugar and cocoa; with on/off motion, cut in butter until in fine crumbs. Mix in egg. Transfer to bowl; knead lightly until dough holds together.

● Press dough onto bottom and sides of greased 10-1/2-inch (27 cm) heart-shaped flan pan; refrigerate.

● BROWNIE FILLING: In bowl set over hot (not boiling) water, melt chocolate; remove from heat. Gradually whisk in butter. Whisk in sugar and vanilla; whisk in eggs, one at a time. Stir in flour, then one-third of the chocolate bars; pour into crust. Bake in 375°F (190°C) oven for 40 minutes or until set but slightly moist in center. Let cool; cover and refrigerate for 8 hours.

● TOPPING: Meanwhile, soften ice cream at room temperature for 20 minutes. Stir in another third of the chocolate bars; freeze. In saucepan over medium-low heat, whisk chocolate with cream until smooth; set aside.

● Forty-five minutes before serving, transfer dessert to platter. Just before serving, scoop ice cream on top; drizzle with chocolate sauce. Sprinkle with remaining chocolate bars. Makes 12 to 15 servings.

Win the hearts of chocolate lovers with this indulgent make-ahead dessert. Need we say more?!

TIP: To bake in an 11-inch (28 cm) round flan pan, decrease baking time by 10 minutes and increase ice cream to 6 cups (1.5 L).

The Contributors

For your easy reference, we have included an alphabetical listing of recipes by contributor.

Bonnie Stern

Lucy Waverman

Canadian Living Test Kitchen

Photography Credits

FRED BIRD: front cover, back cover/background image and bottom right, contents, introduction, 7, 9, 11, 13, 16, 18, 23, 25, 27, 29, 32, 35, 38, 43, 49, 57, 61, 63, 64, 67, 75, 81, 83, 87.

CHRISTOPHER CAMPBELL: back cover/bottom left, 53, 77, 78,

FRANK GRANT: 20, 70,

CURTIS TRENT: front flap.

STANLEY WONG: back cover/upper right, 41.

Special Thanks

Acknowledging the people who have made *Canadian Living's Best Muffins & More* is a pleasure. The creativity, patience and organizing skills of Madison Press project editor Wanda Nowakowska are first in line for appreciation, as are Beverley Renahan, meticulous *Canadian Living* senior editor, and talented pastry chef Daphna Rabinovitch, manager of *Canadian Living's* Test Kitchen. Others at the magazine are due sincere thanks as well: Test Kitchen staff shown on the front flap, plus Donna Bartolini, Jennifer MacKenzie, Dana McCauley, as well as senior editor Donna Paris. Our "looks good enough to eat" photography comes largely via the skills of art director Deborah Fadden, food stylists Olga Truchan and Jennifer McLagan and photographer Fred Bird, and the clean user-friendly design from Gord Sibley. Delicious home baking across Canada is all the more tempting and accessible because of the contributions of *Canadian Living's* very accomplished and valued food writers, noted across the page. Of course, all of our work at *Canadian Living* is under the guidance of editor-in-chief Bonnie Cowan and publisher Kirk Shearer, whose commitment to *The Best* series is wonderful encouragement.

Elizabeth Baird

Index

Over 100 easy-baking favorites that are ready in no time at all.

L

M

N

O

Look to *Canadian Living* for all of THE BEST!

More than 100 quick pasta sauces and tosses, hearty soups, salads and baked entrées, Oriental noodle dishes and vegetarian pasta are featured here in easy-to-follow recipes.

Add some exciting new flavors to your outdoor cooking with the tastiest marinades for meat and fish plus tempting appetizers, vegetables — even pizzas and quesadillas!

More than 100 new ways to cook this family favorite — from skillet suppers and stir-fries to one-pot chicken dinners, soups, salads and dressed-up dishes for company.

Healthy eating is a pleasure when you can enjoy such delicious recipes as *Celery and Sage Pork Roast* and *Buttermilk Mashed Potatoes* with *Strawberry Citrus Charlotte* for dessert.

From sweet to savory to make-ahead mixes — all these muffins take just minutes to prepare. You'll also find easy-to-bake cupcakes, biscuits, cookies and cakes.

Wonderful recipes for satisfying casseroles and stews— along with quick and easy stir-fries, main-course salads and soups, plus super-sized sandwiches and ever popular pasta.

WATCH FOR MORE NEW BOOKS IN THE MONTHS AHEAD... FROM *CANADIAN LIVING* SO YOU KNOW THEY'RE —THE BEST!